To Dave
from
mom
merry Christmas
1992

AMERICA'S DREAM TEAM

America's
Dream Team

The Quest for Olympic Gold

BY COACH CHUCK DALY WITH ALEX SACHARE

NBA

Turner Publishing, Inc.

ATLANTA

USA
BASKETBALL

COPYRIGHT/STAFF CREDITS

Editorial:

ALAN SCHWARTZ
EDITOR-IN-CHIEF

KATHERINE BUTTLER
ASSISTANT EDITOR

MARIAN G. LORD
COPY EDITOR

Design:

MICHAEL J. WALSH
DESIGN DIRECTOR

KAREN E. SMITH
DESIGN AND PRODUCTION

ELAINE STREITHOF
DESIGN AND PRODUCTION

MARTY MOORE
PICTURE RESEARCH

NANCY ROBINS
PRODUCTION DIRECTOR

First Edition 10 9 8 7 6 5 4 3 2 1
Daly, Chuck, with Alex Sachare
America's Dream Team: The Quest for Olympic Gold.
Library of Congress Catalog Card Number: 92-64121
Hardcover: ISBN 1-878685-27-9

Distributed by Andrews and McMeel
4900 Main Street
Kansas City, Missouri 64112

Designed and produced on Macintosh computers using QuarkXpress
and Adobe Photoshop. Color separations and film preparation by
Graphics International, Inc., Atlanta, Georgia.
Printing by R. R. Donnelley, Willard, Ohio.

PREVIOUS PAGES:
MAGIC JOHNSON,
SHOWN ON VIDEO
SCREEN DURING THE
PARADE OF ATHLETES,
WAVES TO THE CROWD
DURING THE OPENING
CEREMONIES OF THE
1992 SUMMER OLYMPIC
GAMES. BARCELONA'S
BASKETBALL ARENA
BECAME THE STAGE
FOR THE FIRST-EVER
PARTICIPATION BY
NBA STARS.

CONTENTS

Chapter One:

THE DREAM FULFILLED 10

Chapter Two:

OLYMPIC HISTORY 18

Chapter Three:

CHOOSING AMERICA'S DREAM TEAM 34

Chapter Four:

THE U.S. OLYMPIC BASKETBALL TEAM 50

Chapter Five:

THE FIRST CHALLENGE 132

Chapter Six:

THE MAGIC OF EARVIN JOHNSON 156

Chapter Seven:

GOING FOR THE GOLD 172

Chapter Eight:

BEYOND BARCELONA 208

STATISTICS 218

ACKNOWLEDGMENTS 224

THE DREAM FULFILLED

I'VE ONLY TASTED champagne in a locker room three times in a coaching career that began in 1955 at Punxsutawney, Pennsylvania, Area Joint High School. The first two occasions were when the Detroit Pistons won NBA titles in 1989 and 1990. The third time was in Barcelona, when we accomplished our goal and won the Olympic gold medal. We only had a little champagne that night, but it tasted very good.

"Dream Team" is a lot of name to live up to, but, if anything, the 1992 U.S. Olympic men's basketball team exceeded all hopes and expectations. I think we truly gave the world a glimpse—only a glimpse, since we were never seriously challenged—of what basketball can be like at its highest level.

Chris Mullin accurately summed up all the elements that had to come together to produce this phenomenon, starting with the decision three years ago to open the Olympics to NBA players. Then he ticked off some more: "How badly we wanted to get back the gold. A number of top players in their prime, and a couple of others at the end of their careers. And everybody willing to throw egos, individual statistics, and all that other stuff out the window to prepare to be the best team ever."

THEIR MISSION ACCOMPLISHED, AMERICA'S DREAM TEAM STANDS ATOP THE VICTORY PLATFORM WHILE "THE STAR-SPANGLED BANNER" IS PLAYED AT THE MEDAL CEREMONY IN BARCELONA.

THE POMP AND PAGEANTRY AT THE OLYMPICS INCLUDE THE PRESENTA-
TION OF THE MEDALS (RIGHT) AND THE RAISING OF THE FLAGS (ABOVE)
AS THE WINNING TEAM'S NATIONAL ANTHEM IS PLAYED.

The one thing I will remember most about this team is the professionalism of the athletes. That's what got us past all the distractions, all the controversies. They wanted to play as a team, put individual statistics aside, and work toward a common goal. A lot of bonding took place among these 12 athletes during the weeks we were together, and it was great to see and be part of.

Many people have asked me, what was I feeling when that final buzzer sounded?

Relief, mainly. This had been a long process, not just seven weeks but almost a year's worth of thought and preparation. There were high expectations and some trepidation. All the players were major stars on their own teams, and as coaches we had some questions as to what would be needed to bring them together. So I felt a form of relief, mixed with joy and a sense of accomplishment, at having put it all together and won the Olympic title.

We finished the way we had begun—with a prayer. Before our first game together in Portland, Michael Jordan said, "Let's say a

prayer, 'Our Father. . . .' " After we beat Croatia in the gold medal game and got back to the locker room, I called everybody together and we said the same prayer. Somehow, it seemed fitting.

Afterward, Magic was asked, "When will there be another Olympic team like this one?" He answered the reporters, "Well, you guys won't be around, and neither will we."

I watched the medal ceremony from the front row of press seats along with my assistant coaches, Lenny Wilkens, Mike Krzyzewski, and P. J. Carlesimo. Only the players get medals and climb up on the victory stand, because the Olympics are supposed to be a celebration of the athletes. At the end of the ceremony, however, Magic Johnson, Charles Barkley, and some of the other guys started waving for us to join them. We declined, because this was their moment, but I was very touched that they wanted to include us in it.

CHARLES BARKLEY, WITH GOLD MEDAL HANGING FROM HIS NECK AND AMERICAN FLAG DRAPED OVER HIS CEREMONY UNIFORM, ACCEPTS CONGRATULATIONS FROM A MEMBER OF THE BRONZE MEDAL-WINNING LITHUANIAN SQUAD.

Some of the players had been on that victory stand before—Michael Jordan, Patrick Ewing, and Chris Mullin were on the 1984 team that won in Los Angeles—but most had never won gold medals. For some, this was their first taste of Olympic victory, and that made it even more special.

I thought there was true joy and true sentiment on that winner's stand, and the players' comments in the locker room afterward really confirmed that. Karl Malone said it was "an awesome feeling, to see 12 athletes come together and do something for their country." David Robinson, who was on the 1988 team that lost in the semifinals and came away from Seoul with a bronze medal, said, "Everything surges up inside you when they play the national anthem. It will be my happiest memory." And Magic said, "It was the most awesome feeling I've ever had winning anything, especially when the national anthem was played. Goose bumps just came all over my body. It's definitely the most exciting thing I've ever been through."

Being with this team was like traveling with 12 rock stars,

that's all I can compare it to. Our every move caused quite a commotion. I'm sure there are some people in Barcelona who are happy we're gone, like the owner of the little restaurant next to our hotel who said his regulars couldn't make it down the street because of all the security surrounding us, but there was real adulation everywhere we went.

The Dream Team was very special in terms of talent, but I think it also was special on a personal level to people around the world—to the French fans who came out at midnight to meet us at the Nice airport, to the UC–San Diego students who waited outside their gym for one of our practices to end so they could see us, and to the many fans in Barcelona who staked out our hotel day and night to watch us come and go. And, of course, it was special to the thousands who saw our games in person and the billions who watched us on television worldwide.

Worldwide interest in the sport is what the International Basketball Federation had in mind when it voted in 1989 to let NBA players participate in the Olympics. Yes, we dominated the tournament, to the point where the only competition was for the silver and bronze medals. And surely we reestablished U.S. dominance in the sport. But I believe we did a lot of good. By capturing people's imagination, the Dream Team gave a big boost to the popularity of basketball around the world. We really won't be able to gauge the overall impact for awhile. But when you have a team with this magnificent talent on TV in roughly 180 countries, before some 3 billion people, it's got to improve the way the game is played.

Out there somewhere was a 12-year-old or a 13-year-old, not necessarily in the United States or in Spain but in any country, who perhaps was seeing these players for the first time. Now that youngster has a dream, and will be willing to work to make that dream come true. And maybe someday that child will get to compete in the Olympics and perhaps win a gold medal.

AFTER HIS TUMUL-
TUOUS YEAR, OLYMPIC
VICTORY MAY NOT
HAVE TASTED SWEET-
ER TO ANYONE THAN
TO MAGIC JOHNSON.

OLYMPIC

LIKE MOST AMERICANS, I took it for granted that the United States was always going to win the gold medal in men's basketball at the Olympics.

After all, basketball is the American game, right?

Wherever you go in the United States you can hear that thump a basketball makes when it's being dribbled—from the blacktop of the city schoolyards in the East to the dirt driveways on the farms of the Midwest to the courts by the beaches of sunny Southern California. We play it one-on-one, three-on-three, five-on-five, half-court or full-court, from the tiniest YMCA gyms to the most magnificent indoor sports palaces. We have the NBA, we have the big college programs. We have Midnight Madness in Kentucky and Hoosier Hysteria in Indiana. It's the American game, invented just over a century ago in Springfield, Massachusetts.

From the time basketball was introduced to the Olympics, as a demonstration sport in St. Louis in 1904 and finally as a medal sport in Berlin in 1936, U.S. teams have dominated the competition. Going into the 1992 Barcelona Olympics, we had compiled an 85–2 record and won nine gold medals.

Early on, that domination was absolute. I can't say I remember us beating Canada 19–8 in 1936 for the first gold medal, but I was only six years old at the time! I do remember the 1956 team,

THE UNIVERSAL PICTURES TEAM, WHICH PLAYED A SCHEDULE OF AMATEUR ATHLETIC UNION BALL, WON THE OLYMPIC TRIALS IN 1936 AND WENT ON TO HELP THE UNITED STATES TO THE FIRST OLYMPIC BASKETBALL GOLD MEDAL IN BERLIN.

HISTORY

led by Bill Russell and K.C. Jones. It overwhelmed everyone at Melbourne, Australia. That team completely demoralized its opponents, winning its games by an incredible average margin of 54 points.

Many consider the 1960 team in Rome, coached by Pete Newell, to be the best amateur team ever assembled. What a roster—Oscar Robertson, Jerry West, Jerry Lucas: three future Hall of Famers. Plus they had four more who would be NBA All-Stars, Walt Bellamy, Bob Boozer, Darrall Imhoff, and Adrian Smith. No wonder they coasted to the gold!

From 1936 to 1956, the United States Olympic team was made up of a combination of collegiate players and those from Amateur Athletic Union teams, players who worked for companies such as Phillips Petroleum or Goodyear Tire and played basketball for the company-sponsored team. In the sixties, most of the players were collegians, but there was still significant AAU

ACTION UNDER THE BASKET AS UNIVERSAL PICTURES BEATS WILMERDING (PENNSYLVANIA) YMCA 42-49 IN THE 1936 OLYMPIC TRIALS IN NEW YORK'S MADISON SQUARE GARDEN.

representation until 1972, when the team came solely from the college ranks.

In 1972, our team averaged just 20.6 years of age, and when we played a team like the Soviet Union it was boys against men. Still, that team was a good one, with several future professionals including Doug Collins, Bobby Jones, Tom Henderson, Dwight Jones, Mike Bantom, Jim Brewer, Tom McMillen, Ed Ratleff, and Tommy Burleson. They won their first eight games, most of them by big scores, including a 68–38 win over Italy in the semi-finals. In the gold medal game they ran into a strong, well-coached, and much older and more experienced team from the Soviet Union.

The Soviet Union led most of the way. With three seconds to play the United States finally pulled ahead 50–49 when Doug Collins drove to the basket, was knocked to the floor by Zurab Sakandelidze, and, though shaken, sank both free throws. The Soviets inbounded the ball, and suddenly play was stopped with one second left. The officials said fans had run onto the court. Play resumed, the Soviets threw the ball off the backboard, the United States team recovered it, and the buzzer sounded as the Americans headed off the court, celebrating a victory.

But after about five minutes, a FIBA official got the United States team out of the locker room and sent it back onto the floor. It seems the Soviet coach had asked for a time-out after Collins's free throws, so three seconds were put back on the clock. The Soviets put the ball in play and missed a shot at the basket, and the American team thought again it had won. But a mistake in setting the game clock caused it to read 50 seconds instead of 3, and so the clock was reset and the ending was replayed once more.

This time the Soviets' Ivan Edeshko hurled a court-length pass to Alexander Belov near the foul line. Belov bumped into Kevin Joyce of the U.S. team, recovered, and shot the ball

CHARLES DARLING (ABOVE, LEFT) BATTLES FOR A LOOSE BALL AGAINST BULGARIA DURING THE 1956 OLYMPICS IN MEL-BOURNE, AUSTRALIA, WHILE (BELOW) 6-9 BILL RUSSELL MEETS SOMEONE HE CAN LOOK UP TO, 7-4 JAN KROUMINCH OF THE SOVIET UNION.

WITH STARS LIKE
JERRY WEST (NO. 3
ABOVE) AND JERRY
LUCAS (NO. 11
BELOW) PLUS OSCAR
ROBERTSON, THE
1960 U.S. OLYMPIC
TEAM DOMINATED
THE COMPETITION
IN ROME, WINNING
BY AN AVERAGE MAR-
GIN OF 42.3 POINTS
PER GAME.

through the hoop for a 51–50 victory. The United States protest-
ed the way the end of the game was conducted, but the protest
was disallowed, and we had suffered our first Olympic defeat.
The U.S. team voted not to accept its silver medals and instead
boarded the next plane home.

Note to the reader: the voice of Alex Sachare, my co-author
and NBA vice president for editorial, is presented in italic type
here and throughout the book, whether he is quoting others or
speaking for himself.

*"I see it today as clearly as if it's happening on a video replay,"
recalled Doug Collins, who went on to a great career with the
Philadelphia 76ers and later became a coach with the Chicago Bulls.
He's now a popular broadcaster doing NBA games on TNT. "It was
a very bittersweet experience for me, to be a member of the first U.S.
men's basketball team to lose in the Olympics, but I still don't believe
that we lost. It was something that was out of our hands.*

*"We were down by one (49–48) with about 10 seconds to go, but I
was able to steal a pass and was heading for a lay-up when I was
fouled with three seconds left. I slid under the basket and hit my head
on the basket support. I was unconscious for a few seconds, and when I*

PETE MCCAFFERY
(NO. 12) LAUNCHES
A JUMPER FOR THE
UNITED STATES
DURING THE 1964
OLYMPICS IN TOYKO.

went to the foul line I still felt groggy. But I think that helped me. I didn't feel the pressure. I made two shots, and we went ahead by one.

"That's when all the confusion began and the Russians got two chances to win it, and they finally put one in and won 51–50. After being so happy about the two free throws I had made, I was the most dejected person in the world.

"Every Olympic year really brings that experience into focus. I think the one thing I regret more than anything else is not having that feeling you get standing on the platform, getting the gold medal around your neck, and listening to the national anthem. I feel we were robbed of that, and that to me is something I really feel badly about."

For many of us, that was truly the first realization that Americans were not the only people playing basketball. In the other Olympics, we had taken it for granted that we would win.

FOR MANY YEARS
THE RUNNING GAME,
A TRADEMARK OF
AMERICAN BASKET-
BALL, GAVE U.S.
OLYMPIC SQUADS
(LIKE THE 1968 TEAM
PICTURED HERE)
AN ADVANTAGE
OVER SLOWER,
MORE MECHANICAL
EUROPEAN TEAMS.

But 1972 sticks in my mind, because that Olympics showed us that we were not invincible. Our dominance had been broken, and the world was catching up.

In 1976 the United States team, coached by Dean Smith, survived an early 95–94 scare at the hands of a Puerto Rican team led by Butch Lee, who played at Marquette and later in the NBA. The U.S. then beat Yugoslavia 95–74 to reclaim the gold

medal. Yugoslavia had defeated the USSR in the semifinals, denying the hoped-for rematch of the heated 1972 finals.

Boycotts affected the next two Olympics. Yugoslavia captured the gold medal in 1980, when the United States boycotted the Moscow Games, and the U.S. team, coached by Bob Knight, beat Spain for the gold in 1984 in Los Angeles, when the Soviet Union boycotted.

Those boycotts were unfortunate, but not surprising. Ideally, there would be no politics in the Olympics. The games would be competitions by the purest of athletes. That was the original thesis, but, obviously, it's not a perfect world.

The first rematch between the United States and the Soviet Union was delayed until the 1988 Olympics in Seoul, Korea.

MIKE SILLIMAN (NO.12, ABOVE) BATTLES FOR A REBOUND FOR THE U.S. SQUAD, WHICH WON ITS SEVENTH CONSECUTIVE GOLD MEDAL IN MEXICO CITY IN 1968.

The teams met in the semifinals, and the Soviet Union, led by future Golden State Warrior Sarunas Marciulionis with 19 points, defeated the United States 82–76. Our team, coached by John Thompson, was weakened by an injury to Hersey Hawkins, which left us without our most effective three-point shooter. The Soviets went on to defeat Yugoslavia for the gold medal. We had to settle for the bronze.

W HEN I STOP AND THINK about it, though, it should not have come as such a shock that the rest of the world was becoming more and more competitive with U.S. basketball teams. Let's face it: we've taught the world how to play the game, starting with their coaches. I've been to Italy seven times and to Spain four times to do clinics myself. We have many, many coaches, collegiate and professional, who travel to other countries all the time.

Then international coaches began coming over here, spend-

THE JOY OF TOM MCMILLEN AND TOM HENDERSON (NOS. 13 AND 6, RIGHT) TURNED TO SORROW AFTER THE FINAL SECONDS OF THE 1972 GOLD MEDAL GAME WERE REPLAYED FOR A SECOND TIME, AND ALEXANDER BELOV SANK THE BASKET (BELOW) THAT GAVE THE SOVIET UNION A 51-50 VICTORY.

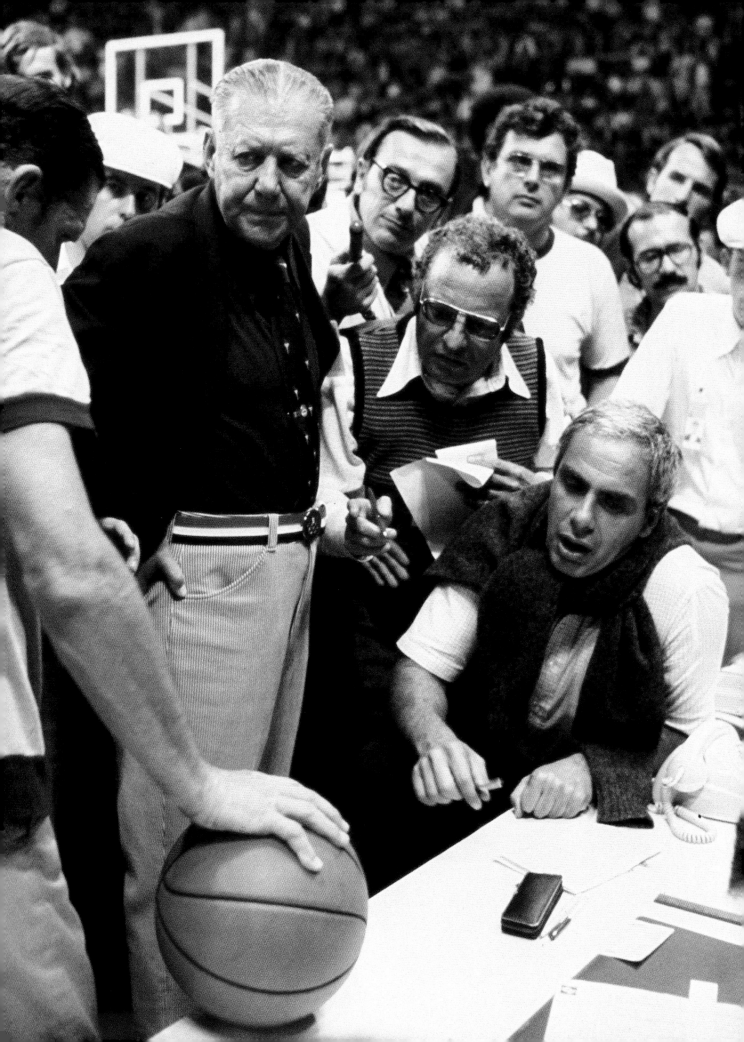

CONFUSION REIGNED
AT THE SCORER'S
TABLE (LEFT) AS OFFI-
CIALS DEBATED THE
CONCLUSION OF
THE 1972 GOLD MEDAL
GAME. IN THE END
IT WAS THE SOVIETS
WHO CELEBRATED
(ABOVE) WHILE
AMERICANS MIKE
BANTOM, JAMES
FORBES, AND ED
RATLEFF (BELOW,
LEFT TO RIGHT)
WERE STUNNED.

ing time with us at our practices—on the collegiate level in particular, but on the professional level, too—learning our game. As
youngsters from other countries began coming to camps and
schools in the United States, it was inevitable that they were
going to develop into good players. They have the athletic ability, and it's a simple game with a rim and a ball. Any player can go
out on his own and play.

For years players from outside the U.S. were more mechanical, less fluid. I guess that came from not having grown up
playing basketball. But they learned how to compensate. For
example, take the three-point shot. They learned how to shoot it
and use it as an effective weapon. They learned the rules and

WILLIE ANDERSON (NO. 10) GOES FOR A JUMP BALL AGAINST BRAZIL'S OSCAR SCHMIDT DURING THE U.S. TEAM'S 102-87 VICTORY IN THE 1988 OLYMPICS AT SEOUL.

how to use them; so while we didn't want to believe that it was going to happen, that others would catch up to us in our own sport, it was really inevitable.

Now there is a generation of kids who have grown up playing basketball. Interest in the sport has exploded all over the world, and particularly in Europe, helped by some of our players who have gone abroad to play professionally.

Most leagues around the world allow two non-citizens—which usually means Americans—to play on their teams, in order to boost the level of play while still keeping the teams predominantly national. The arrival of U.S. pros, many of whom had played in the NBA, began to educate fans to the game, plus their top players got to compete with and against American pros on a regular basis. And as you play against better competition, your level of play automatically increases.

Already world players have become much closer to us in style—much, much closer. They have all the skills. And we're talking about a multitude of countries, not just one or two. So I do think it was inevitable that the rest of the world would catch up—but that didn't make it any less shocking, or upsetting.

The 1989 decision by FIBA to remove restrictions that kept NBA players from participating in major events like the Olympics was long overdue. The United States was the only country whose professional players were not allowed to compete in the Olympics, and that was wrong.

Many people think the United States was behind the move to open the Olympics to NBA players—that it was a knee-jerk reaction to our loss to the Soviets in the 1988 Olympics. Actually, just the opposite is true.

"The NBA's position was that they didn't want to be a part of it," said Dave Gavitt, president of USA Basketball and senior executive VP of the Boston Celtics. "The NBA never lobbied for it. They didn't want to be tagged as the guys coming in to take over the Olympics."

It was the rest of the world that wanted to get NBA players into the Olympics, and in fact the movement had been gaining momentum for years, even before the loss to the Soviets in the 1988 games. Actually, the man behind it was Boris Stankovic, FIBA's highly respected secretary general from Yugoslavia and a man with a true global vision for the sport of basketball.

"The best going against the best, that is the ideal situation. That's the only way to make progress in world basketball," said Stankovic, who in the mid-1980s began pushing to open the Olympics to all. The issue came up for a vote at the FIBA Congress held in conjunction with the 1986 World Championships but lost by a narrow 31–27 margin.

Stymied in his bid to open the 1988 Olympics to NBA players, Stankovic continued to work to unify the sport on a global scale. He joined with David Stern, the forward-thinking commissioner of the NBA, to create the McDonald's Open, the first FIBA-sanctioned tournament that included both NBA and foreign teams. The tournament was inaugurated in Milwaukee in 1987, where the NBA's Milwaukee Bucks won in a round-robin against the Soviet National Team and Tracer Milan, the Italian club team that was the reigning European champion. Since then the McDonald's Open has been held in Madrid, Rome, Barcelona, and Paris, and has become one of the biggest sport-

LED BY FUTURE GOLDEN STATE WARRIOR SARUNAS MARCIULIONIS (NO. 7), THE SOVIET UNION BEAT THE UNITED STATES 82-76 EN ROUTE TO THE GOLD IN 1988.

AN INJURY TO HERSEY
HAWKINS (NO. 7
RIGHT) LEFT THE 1988
U.S. TEAM, COACHED
BY JOHN THOMPSON
(ABOVE), WITHOUT
ITS BEST OUTSIDE
SHOOTER AND VUL-
NERABLE TO THE
SOVIET UNION'S
PACKED-IN DEFENSE.

ing events in Europe. Stankovic's dream, however, was to get NBA players into the Olympics.

"The first reason I want this is technical, to improve the skills of our [FIBA] players," argued Stankovic. "The second is moral. We now have a very hypocritical situation. We have 172 countries in our organization representing 200 million basketball players, but we do not have the best 300 players in the world because they are 'professionals.' People are being paid all over the world. To leave out the best 300 players because they have the name of professionals is hypocritical."

Stankovic was supported by Juan Antonio Samaranch, the president of the International Olympic Committee and a native of Barcelona, Spain, site of the 1992 Olympics. The issue was again brought to a vote by FIBA in 1989, and this time it passed by an overwhelming 56–13 margin.

"We see this as our triumphant entry into the 21st century," said Stankovic. "It is a dream come true.

"We accept the fact that the Olympics and World Championships will be dominated by the United States, but that difference will be less every year. And one of these years, other countries will be competitive with the NBA.

"Remember that from 1936 to 1972, the target for all other nations in Olympic basketball was second place. Since 1972 it has not been so, and it will be the same pattern now. Right now the United States is certainly the strongest, but the world will catch up."

I agree that the rest of the world is closing the gap, and there's no question in my mind that they're going about it in a very intelligent way. Having NBA players in the Olympics is going to make all the countries better over the long haul.

Frankly, having watched the European championships in 1991, I saw teams like Yugoslavia that were not that far away from being competitive. A gold medal game against Yugoslavia, had their country stayed unified, would have been a game to remember for a long, long time.

CHOOSING AMERICA'S DREAM TEAM

DAVE GAVITT, the president of USA Basketball, laid down the gauntlet for me even before a single player had been named to the U.S. Olympic team.

"This will be the most powerful basketball team ever put together," he predicted back in September 1990, and with those words he made my responsibility perfectly clear: Bring home the gold medal. Period. Nothing less. If we didn't do that, we might as well stay in Barcelona and not come home again—or retire to the country that beat us!

Nevertheless, it was a challenge I eagerly embraced. Coaching the United States Olympic Team—Men's Basketball is the ultimate honor for me, the culmination of more than 30 years in this business, and I wanted to win the gold medal for the USA. I'm a lifer, a basketball guy. We have the greatest coaches and the greatest players, and I hope we've shown it to the world.

But with all the great players in the NBA, not to mention the college ranks, how do you pick a 12-man team? No matter who you choose, some outstanding individuals are going to be left off. Picking this team was an impossible task, and I did not envy the group that had to do it.

Many people don't realize that in the 1992 Olympic Games, the coach did not select the U.S. Olympic team, and had very

WHO WOULD FILL THE UNIFORMS OF AMERICA'S DREAM TEAM?
SELECTING THE DOZEN PLAYERS WAS NO SIMPLE TASK.

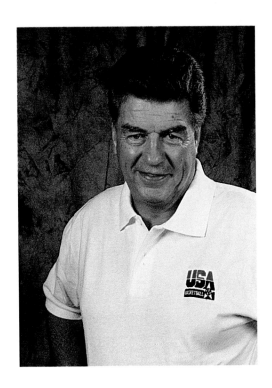

ALTHOUGH DALY
WAS HEAD COACH
OF THE U.S. OLYMPIC
TEAM, HE WAS NOT
A MEMBER OF THE
COMMITTEE THAT
SELECTED THE
PLAYERS.

little input. This is different from past years, when the coach played a major role in the selection process. But this year the team was selected by one of the USA Basketball Committees, known as the Men's Olympic Team Subset. It originally consisted of 13 voting members:

C. M. Newton, *Athletic Director, University of Kentucky (Chair)*

Wayne Embry, *VP/General Manager, Cleveland Cavaliers (Vice Chair)*

Bob Bass, *Head Coach/VP of Basketball Operations, San Antonio Spurs*

Quinn Buckner, *Former U.S. Olympic athlete and broadcaster*

P. J. Carlesimo, *Head Coach, Seton Hall University*

Bill Cunningham, *Partner, Miami Heat*

Charles Grantham, *Executive Director, National Basketball Players Association*

Mike Krzyzewski, *Head Coach, Duke University*

Jack McCloskey, *General Manager, Detroit Pistons*

George Raveling, *Head Coach, University of Southern California*

Rod Thorn, *Vice President, Operations, National Basketball Association*

Jan Volk, *Executive VP and General Manager, Boston Celtics*

Donnie Walsh, *President, Indiana Pacers*

Buckner and McCloskey withdrew from the committee during the period when the team was being chosen, and Willis Reed, vice president of basketball operations for the New Jersey Nets, was added as a replacement.

This was a very solid group of basketball people who were committed to making the right decisions for the right reasons. Obviously, just about anybody you talk to is going to disagree about one or two players, but that's understandable. You're never going to get total agreement on the makeup of a team like this one. You just have to accept that fact and go on from there.

"The head coach and the coaching staff played an advisory role in the selection process," explained C. M. Newton, who chaired the Selection Committee. "We selected the coach and the coaching staff first, of course, and then we asked Chuck and his staff what they wanted in the makeup of the team. We asked them, 'How do you intend to play?

How do you intend to cover the other teams' three-point shooters, for example? What kind of team do you want?' Basically, we asked for their guidance in selecting the team.

"The other thing that we asked Chuck was, 'Do you want any specialty people? Is there anything unusual you want us to look at?' The thing Chuck said he wanted was flexibility, and as we ranked the NBA players we saw we had that. Magic Johnson can play many positions, so can Michael Jordan, Scottie Pippen, and several others. Flexibility is critical for an Olympic team because once we get to Barcelona, we can't substitute. If somebody gets hurt, you play a man short. So it's vital to have players who can play multiple positions."

A frequent question was, why not have the coach play a more active role in the selection process?

"Oh, I don't know, I guess for the political aspects," said Newton. "Certainly the coach's input is wanted, and the committee members are

THE FIRST 10
MEMBERS WERE
ANNOUNCED
DURING AN NBC
SPECIAL BROADCAST
FROM NBA ENTER-
TAINMENT'S STUDIO
IN SECAUCUS, N.J.

THE CHANCE TO
WEAR THE USA BAS-
KETBALL UNIFORM
WAS SOMETHING NO
PLAYER COULD TURN
DOWN. AND THE
CHANCE TO COACH
THIS TEAM WAS, FOR
DALY, "A NO-BRAINER."

going to be sensitive to what the coach wants. But if he were to make the selections, you put an active coach in a very difficult position. By keeping him in an advisory capacity, you try to take some of the pressure off him."

In reality, that attempt didn't totally work. Even though I didn't pick the team, I still took some heat over the selections. Obviously there are both advantages and disadvantages to having a committee pick the Olympic team in men's basketball, rather than the head coach or the coaching staff.

On the one hand, every coach likes to pick his players. Because certain players are better suited for one style of play than another, a coach is going to take players whose talents match the kind of game he prefers. Also, from the standpoint of personalities, it's helpful for a coach to have players with whom he's familiar and who know his style and his preferences.

On the other hand, having the committee pick the players did relieve me of some, even if not all, criticism in the area of player selection. That's a big plus, especially if you're going to announce the bulk of the team in September and then go through an entire NBA season before bringing everybody together for the run to the Olympic Games.

Let's suppose that I, as the coach, were allowed to pick four players. Then every player who felt he should have made the team will come into our arena with the attitude, "How dare you leave me off the team? I'll show you how good I am!" That's too tough a position in which to put any coach.

Much of the heat that I did take revolved around my own team. We had three players on the Detroit Pistons—Isiah Thomas, Joe Dumars, and Dennis Rodman—who certainly were of Olympic and All-Star caliber, and I know each was very disappointed when the first 10 players were announced and he was not on the list.

The big controversy swirled around Isiah, whose credentials

DALY JOINS USA BASKETBALL PRESIDENT DAVE GAVITT (LEFT) AND NBC
BROADCASTER BOB COSTAS (RIGHT) FOR THE ANNOUNCEMENT OF THE
FIRST 10 PLAYERS ON AMERICA'S DREAM TEAM.

definitely are impressive—he was the key player in the Pistons' rise, the team's playmaker and captain, a proven winner and one of the great point guards in the game. But how about Joe and Dennis? Joe plays both ends of the court as well as anyone, and you're never going to meet a classier individual; while Dennis led the league in rebounding and is among the league's best defensive players. Any of these three could have been named to the team. I would have loved to have had them, and nobody would have said they didn't deserve it. The same goes for some of the other great players around the league, guys like Reggie Miller, Dominique Wilkins, James Worthy, Tim Hardaway, Kevin Johnson—I could go on and on.

So, how did the committee go about selecting America's Dream Team?

First of all, it was decided that the old method of conducting Olympic Trials would not work. What sense would it make to invite Michael Jordan or Magic Johnson to a one-week tryout period? Everyone knows what they can do! Also, there was a limit as to how much time these players could be asked to give up over the course of a summer. So they decided to forget about holding trials and, instead, to select a group of players and extend invitations to them.

"The Olympic Trials worked when it was a college team," explained Newton, "because there's always somebody out there at some school that you don't know about. Dan Majerle is a perfect example; he didn't have much of a national reputation when he made the 1988 Olympic team out of Central Michigan. We felt that this time, with a predominantly pro team, there would be no one out there that we wouldn't know. So what we did, essentially, is take the last two NBA seasons, plus college seasons, and use them as our Olympic Trials."

The committee asked that I meet with them in Orlando on April 7, 1991. I didn't know what to expect, but I did prepare a list of players at each position, roughly six or seven players in

alphabetical order, to have something to work from. I knew it was not going to be easy. I mean, I looked at the list and said, "How can you pick a team from this list? How can you leave any of these guys off?"

I could see it was going to be a difficult process. Things went very slowly, and I think the committee left that meeting with five or six guys who would be on the team, the obvious guys. That was the only face-to-face meeting I had with the committee, although there were some conference calls after that.

Another complication was, nobody knew that everybody invited was going to accept. I had been through two championship seasons and a third trip to the Finals, and I knew how we all felt in June—like you'd gotten hit by a truck, or worse. So, would everybody want to play? We didn't know.

Picking the players for the USA Basketball team was indeed no easy task.

"Trying to name 10 players is ultimately unsatisfying, when you consider that we choose 24 players for the NBA All-Star Game and many great ones don't make it," said NBA Deputy Commissioner Russ Granik, who serves as vice president of USA Basketball and was a nonvoting member of the committee. "Everybody can't make the team. There are many deserving players who won't be on the team. There just isn't much we can do about it."

Faced with that reality, the committee held two meetings and several conference calls, after which it announced on September 13, 1991, the first 10 members of the USA Basketball team:

Charles Barkley	Karl Malone
Larry Bird	Chris Mullin
Patrick Ewing	Scottie Pippen
Magic Johnson	David Robinson
Michael Jordan	John Stockton

It also announced that it would name the remaining team members, at least one of whom would come from the college ranks, after the completion of the 1991–92 NCAA and NBA seasons.

Rod Thorn, another key member of the USAB's selection committee, is the NBA's hands-on basketball expert, a star player in high school and college whose pro career was hampered by injury and who later served as both a coach and general manager. It was in the latter capacity that he drafted a player by the name of Michael Jordan for the Chicago Bulls in 1984.

"At our meeting in Orlando, Chuck brought along a list of players he felt were of the caliber that should be considered for the team," said Thorn. "It was a long list, with all the names you'd expect to see on such a list. There were no surprises on it. However, we were not ready at that point to start selecting players. After the meeting ended, I went back and spoke with a lot of people and then prepared another list of players, which, not surprisingly, turned out to be similar to the one

JAZZ STARS KARL MALONE AND JOHN STOCKTON WERE UNABLE TO ATTEND THE NBC SELECTION SHOW IN NEW JERSEY, SO THE NETWORK SENT A CAMERA CREW TO THEM IN UTAH.

Chuck had. So that was where we began."

Newton picks it up from there. "We took that long list and shortened it to the point where we had about five players at each position. That was rough, but shortening the list further was even rougher. When we finally settled on 10 players, we decided to go to those 10 and find out if they would play.

"Another thing the committee spent a lot of time doing was setting up the expectations for the players—the time commitment, the training facilities, and so forth—so they would understand exactly what was involved. Then the determination was made to have Russ Granik and Rod Thorn of the NBA go directly to the players, tell them what the expectations were, and find out if they would accept were they to be selected.

"Each player who was contacted said yes, and I felt that was really strong. If you remember, when we were going into this, a lot of people said we would never get this guy to play or that guy to play. But every player just jumped right on it."

"These guys are basketball players," noted Granik. "That's what they do, they're proud of what they do, and this was a chance to do something historic."

The committee's job was not yet finished. Two more players were still to be named to complete the team, after the conclusion of the 1991–92 NBA and college seasons. The idea was to leave a couple of spots on

the squad open, so that a player who might come on strong in '92—either in the pros or in college—would not be precluded from consideration for a place on the team.

By the time the committee gathered at the Basketball Hall of Fame enshrinement ceremonies in Springfield, Massachusetts, on May 11, there had been much speculation about who the choices would be. But the first decision was a procedural one: the committee decided to add one NBA player and one from the college ranks, the feeling being strong among some committee members that there should be at least one non-NBA player on the squad. Then it came time to discuss names.

"There were several players, as you can imagine, who were considered for both spots," said Newton. "We took several ballots on the different selections."

Two names stood out: Clyde Drexler of the Portland Trail Blazers and Christian Laettner of Duke University.

NBC BROADCASTER MARV ALBERT (RIGHT) INTERVIEWS MAGIC JOHNSON, WHO WAS DRESSED SOMEWHAT MORE FORMALLY THAN HE WOULD BE IN THE OLYMPICS.

CHOOSING THE COACHES

At a meeting in Boca Raton, Florida, on September 13, 1990, the selection committee came up with the following prerequisites for the Olympic coaching staff:

•Head Coach: eight years coaching experience, including at least three years as an NBA head coach; active NBA head coach in at least two of the last three seasons.

•Assistant Coaches: one active NBA head coach; other two must be active Division I college head coaches with at least five years of college and/or pro experience and previous international experience.

It also was stipulated that the coach must have no conflict of interest, as determined by USA Basketball, and would be chosen with regard to "character, tact, disciplinary judgment, sense of responsibility, knowledge of basketball and other special qualifications," according to a form submitted by USAB to FIBA on January 15, 1991.

"The committee spent long hours talking about the criteria for coach selection," said Newton. "Since we were going to be a predominantly NBA team, it was determined that we have an NBA coach as the head coach, as well as another NBA head coach as one of the assistants. But since we were also going to have college representation, we decided to have two college Division I head coaches with previous international experience as assistants."

What made Daly appealing to the committee?

"Chuck is someone who brings great qualifications to the job," said Dave Gavitt, the president of USA Basketball. "He has had outstanding coaching careers at the high school and college levels and is one of the premier NBA head coaches. He is someone who reflects the

THE CHALLENGE OF MOLDING 12 INDIVIDUAL STARS INTO AN EFFECTIVE UNIT WAS ENTRUSTED TO A COACHING STAFF OF (LEFT TO RIGHT): P. J. CARLESIMO, MIKE KRZYZEWSKI, CHUCK DALY, AND LENNY WILKENS.

high level of expertise of our previous Olympic coaches."

"Obviously, Chuck's success in the NBA was very important," added Newton. *"One thing that appealed to me personally is that he's coached at every level. I felt that in particular with these Olympics, where we are in such change, it would be really good to have somebody who has paid his dues at each level.*

"Another thing that was important to me was that I wanted someone about whom the players would say, 'Yeah, I'd like to play for him.' I thought Chuck commanded that respect. He's a player's coach, and that's important because it's the players, not the coach, who will be out there."

What tipped the choice in my favor?

I think that the committee looked first at where I'd come from. I was a lifer. I'd coached on every level—high school, collegiate, and professional. I'd crossed all the boundaries in terms of coaching. I think, next, they looked at our accomplishments in Detroit, the fact that our team had won two championships and been in a third NBA finals. I had been successful—but I don't think our record was the paramount reason I was selected.

There was some discussion about my being a guy who can deal with players, a "player's coach." Well, sometimes yes, sometimes no! But I think that's part of being a successful professional coach today. Everybody in the business knows the game of basketball and what to do in a given situation—it's not rocket science we're talking about. But there are some things you have to do as a coach that are important.

First of all, you have to look at your personnel and see what they are able to do offensively and defensively. That's No. 1 on the professional level. Systems are nice, but I think it's better to suit systems to personnel than vice versa. You have to learn to take advantage of the personnel that you are given as a coach.

Also, in this day and age, the people aspect of coaching is paramount. A coach to a great degree has to be a people person.

AFTER A TOUGH PRACTICE, COACH DALY PONDERS THE TASK AHEAD.

That doesn't mean he has to give up all discipline, but he does have to give up some of it. He has to be willing to go the last mile. I remember listening to John Wooden at a clinic, it seems like 100 years ago, and he made a statement I'll never forget. He said, "When I was a young coach, I didn't go the last mile. But as I've grown in my profession, I've learned how to go the last mile for a player."

To be a successful coach in the NBA, you must understand the mentality of the players, how difficult it is to play four or five games a week over the course of a season, and not go off the deep end as a coach every time you lose. We are dealing with the highest level of athlete. You can't pound them hard in practice and hope that they will be able to play at their best in a game.

With the U.S. Team coming together for several extra weeks of basketball after a long season, there was no way we could go to two-a-days or anything of that nature. This had to be not only a basketball experience but a social experience, and it had to be enjoyable or we were going to lose some of these people mentally as well as physically.

When choosing the rest of the staff, "we had similar discussions about the assistants as we had about the head coach," said Newton. "Then we went to Chuck and he was fine with the people we chose.

"Lenny Wilkens is a long-time NBA head coach with a proven record of success, and Chuck was very enthusiastic about having him as one of the assistants. Mike Krzyzewski of Duke and P. J. Carlesimo of Seton Hall have been successful Division I head coaches, and both have coached internationally in recent years. We thought that was essential, because just as the pro game is different from college, the international game is different, too: the game is 40 minutes long instead of 48, there's a 30-second clock instead of 24, the lane is different, the three-point shot plays a much greater role, zone defenses are allowed. Also, Mike and P. J. are familiar with the personnel in other countries from having coached against them."

THE U.S. OLYMPIC BASKETBALL TEAM

THERE IS WOOD EVERYWHERE at Chuck Daly's Great Northern, much of it bare, some lacquered, some painted green in a color scheme designed to bring the great outdoors of northern Michigan into the restaurant on Orchard Lake Road in West Bloomfield, a tony suburb north of Detroit. Moose and elk heads watch over patrons who dine on such specialties as Great Northern bean soup, broiled Lake Superior whitefish, and smoked pork chops trucked down from Plath's in Rogers City, Michigan (the only place for smoked pork chops, according to the locals). A large canoe and murals of marshlands adorn the bar area, where the only concession to the 1990s are a couple of arcade games along the wall. There is a comfortable feeling of time-lessness, of the expansive dining room of a rural hunting and fishing lodge that will not have changed much from the 19th century to the 21st.

About the only connection to the primary profession of the eatery's namesake is a small enclosure with hardwood floor and fiberglass backboard, where patrons can practice their free-throw shooting while waiting for the catch of the day to find its way to their tables.

Otherwise, you might think Chuck Daly was the host of one of those fishing shows on the cable sports stations, or perhaps a former sidekick of Curt Gowdy's on the old "American Sportsman" series.

Business is brisk on on this chilly Wednesday afternoon in mid-February as Daly walks in and doffs his hat and coat to reveal a stylish running suit and sneakers, the kind of leisure outfit you'd expect from a basketball coach with two NBA championship rings to his credit. The 62-year-old Daly works the room, moving from table to table, shaking hands and welcoming the lunchtime crowd. He does this a few times each week as part of his deal with the restaurant chain backing this venture.

Finally he settles in at a table in the bar area, just to the side of the foul shooting court, orders chicken salad in a pita, and discusses the players he'll be coaching on the Men's U.S. Olympic Basketball Team. He's still a bit surprised by the role he's going to play:

Coaching this team is an overwhelming honor for a guy who's been in basketball some 35-plus years. It's the honor of all honors. I'll see a report on TV, and they'll say, "Chuck Daly, the Olympic coach..." and I still can't comprehend it. I'll see it and say, "Oh, yeah, is that really me?"

Representing your country is an honor that's hard to describe. It's something you dream of, never knowing if you'll be lucky enough to get the chance. And when that chance comes, the decision is a no-brainer. There are no hesitations, no second thoughts about this job—you take it. The honor, the challenge, the possibility of working with this amount of talent is something that's not going to happen to a lot of people in our profession.

There's no question in my mind that I'll be coaching what may be the greatest array of stars ever assembled—which doesn't necessarily mean the greatest team. That will be the primary challenge facing the four coaches: to try, in a very short period of time, to bring this group together as a team.

I do know that our players can adapt. I coached an NBA All-

Star Game in 1990, and I was stunned by how they accepted what we wanted to do, how they were able to handle it. There is so much respect among players at this level for each other's ability that sometimes they over-pass, not wanting to step on each other's toes.

One thing all of these people have in common is intelligence. Is there a correlation between superior athletes and superior intelligence? I don't know. I do know that all the people on this team are very, very intelligent about the game. I don't know about book learning or computers or all of that, but these guys are brilliant in their field, which is basketball. And they never stop working. We've got a lot of guys in every sport who stop working once they reach the pros, once they receive their first contract, once they attain a certain level. Then there are the guys who are willing to work on their bodies, develop new kinds of shots, new defensive skills, move up to a different level. And those are the kind of players we have. Each of them is constantly working on his game, striving to eliminate any weaknesses and enhance his strengths. It takes that kind of effort and dedication to climb to the top of any profession, which is where these athletes stand.

It's going to be important for us to devise a system that's relatively simple, to take advantage of the talent, and still be able to get in some form of organization both offensively and defensively in a short period of time. We're going to have to make some hard decisions, particularly with regard to playing time, because you can't have all 12 guys play the number of minutes they're used to playing. These decisions are not going to be popular with some people. That's part of our challenge as coaches—to get the players to accept what we're trying to do and the way we are going about it.

But there's no question about the individual talent. These players are the best.

M OST PEOPLE KNOW Charles Barkley, All-NBA forward of the Phoenix Suns, only through his fierce on-court persona, and the seemingly endless string of controversies that swirl around him. They might be surprised to learn that every summer he returns to his hometown of Leeds, Alabama, where he visits his mother, grandmother, and two brothers in a house he rebuilt for them after he made it to the NBA with the Philadelphia 76ers in 1984.

"I think the greatest satisfaction I get out of playing in the NBA and making a lot of money is being able to do things for my family," said Barkley. "When I rebuilt the house and bought them cars, it was a great feeling. My mother and grandmother taught me the value of working hard, and that's the key to being successful."

"He always had time to talk to me, and he always had time to listen to me," said his mother, Charcey Glenn. "He did a lot of things he didn't have to do. He took a lot of burdens off me. A lot of times I had to work two jobs, so when I came home, Charles would have the house cleaned up from top to bottom. For a long time, he was not only a big brother to Darryl and John Derrick but also a father figure. He always stuck up for his brothers and looked after them."

Barkley spent much time with his grandmother when he was growing up, and they remain close.

"Granny showed me how to speak up for myself," said Barkley. "That's why I'm such an honest person. If I upset some people, then so be it. I'm not going to apologize for being honest."

"Sometimes I wish he wouldn't talk so much!" replies his

"PLAYING IN THE OLYMPICS IS A GREAT OPPORTUNITY. IT'S NOT OFTEN YOU HAVE A CHANCE TO MAKE HISTORY. NO MATTER HOW MANY TEAMS GO IN THE FUTURE THE FIRST ONE IS SPECIAL. IT WILL ALWAYS BE THE ANSWER TO A TRIVIA QUESTION!"

BARKLEY

grandmother, Johnnie Mae Edwards. "He'll always say, 'Granny, when I was growing up you always told me to tell the truth, and now you're telling me to keep my mouth shut.' I tell him, 'You're old enough to know when to tell the truth and when to keep your mouth shut.'"

Barkley, who was described by Philadelphia Inquirer *sports columnist Bill Lyon as "a raging, unique talent and a many-splendored entertainer," rarely keeps his mouth shut. Everything about him is loud and bold, from his basketball virtuosity to his brash verbosity. He is a burst of neon amidst a background of pastel, a crash of cymbals amidst a chorus of flutes. There is no stopping "Sir Charles," on or off the court.*

Charles is the Damon Runyon character of our league, larger than life. The guy is fun. As long as you don't have to deal with him every day, he's great. He's an MVP candidate, but he also could probably start the Third World War!

As a player, what can't he do? He shoots threes and he can take the ball end to end. Other than Karl Malone, he's probably the most powerful guy in the game today. He draws double-teams every time he has the ball, and he knows how to beat them.

Sure he can be a little difficult, but controversy is sometimes interesting. When you lose characters, I think you lose visibility for the sport. Players like Charles are good for the game, as long as you keep it under some kind of control. Sometimes he crosses the line, that's true. But he's an individual, and it's the American way to say what you want, particularly when you can back it up on the court as he does.

I'm looking forward to coaching him. He's a great player, a proud athlete who wants very much to win, and his frustrations come from not winning. It's tough to lose year after year. And I'm concerned about him physically, because he takes a beating every night and that has to take its toll over the years.

I think Charles will be fun for the team. And I think the players on this team will have so much respect for each other,

ONE OF BASKET-
BALL'S FREE SPIRITS,
THERE'S NO
STOPPING CHARLES
BARKLEY—ON OR
OFF THE COURT.

BARKLEY, GUARDING
MICHAEL JORDAN
ABOVE, WAS THE
STAR OF STARS IN
1991 WHEN HE
SCORED 17 POINTS
AND GRABBED 22
REBOUNDS TO EARN
MVP HONORS IN THE
NBA ALL-STAR GAME.

that will help us as a coaching staff. It's not like having one star who overshadows everybody else on the team. And no one player will have to carry the load for us, because every one of our players is a go-to guy. Any one of them is fully capable of stepping up on a given night and giving us what we need. Here the status and physical skills of each member should balance out very nicely. I think everyone may be surprised at how willing these players will be to compromise their individual games for the good of the team.

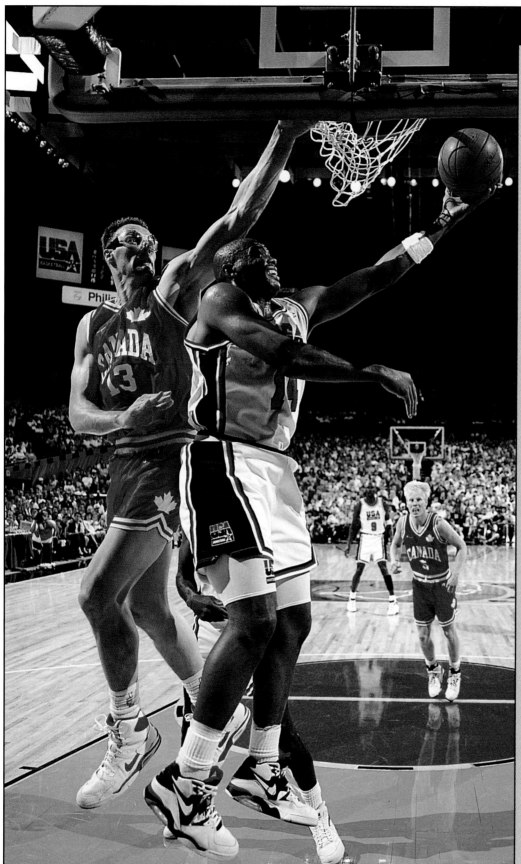

CHARLES WADE BARKLEY

Forward

Phoenix Suns

6-6, 252, 29 years old
Birthdate: February 20, 1963
High School: Leeds, Alabama
College: Auburn

• Eight-year NBA veteran.

• Six-time NBA All-Star.

• All-Star Game Most
Valuable Player, 1991.

• All-NBA First Team four
consecutive seasons (1988
through 1991), Second
Team three times (1986,
1987 and 1992).

• Winner of Schick Award
for overall contributions
to team's success three
straight seasons (1986
through 1988).

• All-Rookie Team, 1985.

• Led NBA in rebounding,
1987.

• Led Philadelphia 76ers in
scoring and rebounding six
straight seasons (1987
through 1992).

• Leads all active players in
field goal percentage, .576.

• NBA career averages:
23.3 points, 11.6 rebounds,
3.7 assists.

GROWING UP IN FRENCH LICK, a rural Indiana town with a population just over 2,000, Larry Bird was introduced to the game of basketball by older brothers Mike and Mark. When Larry started high school, Mark was the star of the Springs Valley team. "I could see he was proud of how he played, and I wanted the same thing," recalled Bird.

Success did not come easily. It was the product of hard work, determination, and endless hours of practice.

"He was just an average basketball player at that time," said Springs Valley teammate Tony Clark. "But there used to be a basketball court halfway up a hill, and I can remember seeing Larry out there shooting a basketball in the rain, practicing by himself."

"I had a couple of friends I used to play with a lot, and I was picking up on things I thought were relatively simple moves and they were having a hard time with them. That's when things started clicking for me," said Bird.

He devoted himself to the game as he grew from 6-1 as a high school sophomore to 6-7 as a senior, by which time he was averaging 30 points and 20 rebounds a game.

"We didn't have a lot when I was growing up," he reflected. "Basketball, when it came into my life—that's all I did."

Bird, widely recruited, chose to attend Indiana University but quickly became homesick and dropped out. A year later he enrolled at

"THIS IS GOING FOR THE GOLD, AND I NEVER HAD THE CHANCE BEFORE. I'LL GET TO PLAY WITH ALL THESE GREAT PLAYERS THAT I HAVEN'T HAD THE CHANCE TO PLAY WITH. I'LL PROBABLY BE MORE EXCITED THAN ANYONE."

BIRD

Indiana State in Terre Haute, whose small-town atmosphere was more to his liking. Bird turned the unheralded Indiana State Sycamores into a national power, leading them to the 1979 NCAA Finals, where they suffered their only defeat of the season at the hands of Magic Johnson and Michigan State.

Bird, now a 6-9, 220-pounder who could shoot and pass like a guard, joined the Boston Celtics and keyed the resurrection of their fallen dynasty, winning Rookie of the Year honors in 1980 and leading the green and white to NBA championships in 1981, 1984, and 1986. He became a perennial NBA All-Star and was the league's MVP in 1984, 1985, and 1986.

Besides being a great shooter and passer, a solid rebounder, a savvy defensive player, and a no-holds-barred competitor, Bird has an innate feel for the game, the basketball instinct to know how a play will unfold long before anyone else.

"He has this uncanny sense about the game," said Celtics Coach Chris Ford, who played with Bird for three seasons. "He'll do things out there that just leave you shaking your head and smiling. And he created this unselfish attitude on the team."

"When you've got a Bird out there," said Hall of Fame guard Bob Cousy, now a Celtics broadcaster, "the other four guys know if they just move and get in the right place, the ball is going to be there. It's beautiful. You get four other guys over-achieving. He makes them better basketball players."

"If I had to start a team today," Celtics President Red Auerbach, the winningest coach in NBA history, said when Bird was in his prime, "the one guy I would take would be Larry Bird."

Larry Bird is a coach's player. There are certain players that appeal to a coach's mentality. Bird, more so than even most of the others on the Olympic team, has the ability to make those around him better. His feel for the game, his feel for passing, is extraordinary. And you want to talk about shooting? He's the king of the three-point shooters. Physically, he's a very powerful, strong

LARRY BIRD'S BLUE-COLLAR WORK ETHIC DEFINED HIS APPROACH TO BASKETBALL; DIVING TO THE FLOOR FOR LOOSE BALLS WAS ALL PART OF THE GAME FOR THE INDIANA NATIVE.

WITH A CLASSIC
SHOOTING FORM
THAT NEVER VARIED
THROUGH THE
YEARS, BIRD WON
THE CHEERS OF
CELTICS FANS AT
BOSTON GARDEN.

guy, but he's the ultimate team player, the ultimate professional.

His real genius is his knowledge of the game, his understanding of when and how to distribute the ball. He's so clever defensively, the way he reads teams, anticipates plays, makes steals. I don't know if there's anyone who has made more big plays than he has.

The play he made against us [stealing an inbounds pass from Isiah Thomas in the closing seconds of Game 5 of the 1987 NBA Playoffs, then passing to Dennis Johnson for the game-winning lay-up] might have been the single greatest play I've ever seen. Not only did he make the steal, but the pass to Dennis Johnson was so incredible, I'll never forget it. I got home that night and I was still speechless. I know he's made a lot of great plays, but that one will go down in history.

It's almost an impossible play! Most guys, even if they somehow make the steal, they catch the ball and look around and before they can do anything with it the game is over. Not Bird—he knew what he was going to do with the ball even before he made the steal.

Every time we turn on the TVs here in the restaurant, that play is on the NBA video. It's a constant reminder of his greatness.

LARRY
JOE
BIRD

Forward

Boston Celtics

6-9, 220, 35 years old

Birthdate: December 7, 1956

High School: Springs Valley,

French Lick, Indiana

College: Indiana State

• 13-year NBA veteran.

• 12-time NBA All-Star.

• NBA Most Valuable Player

three straight seasons

(1984 through 1986).

• NBA Finals Most Valuable

Player twice (1984 and 1986).

• All-Star Game Most

Valuable Player, 1982.

• All-NBA First Team nine

straight seasons (1980

through 1988), Second

Team once (1990).

• Rookie of the Year and

All-Rookie Team, 1980.

• Led Boston Celtics to three

NBA World Championships

(1981, 1984 and 1986).

• Led NBA in free throw

percentage four times (1984,

1986, 1987 and 1990).

• NBA career averages:

24.3 points, 10.0 rebounds,

6.3 assists.

PORTLAND TRAIL BLAZERS—GUARD/FORWARD

IN CLYDE DREXLER'S CASE, the nickname is oh, so appropriate. Clyde "the Glide" Drexler has soared to the top of the basketball world the same way he soars to the basket—smoothly, with quiet efficiency and no wasted effort. A six-time All-Star and an All-NBA First Team selection, he glides through the league without stirring the waters, letting his game speak for him; that he does so in the relatively small market of Portland, Oregon, only adds to his image as the NBA's quiet superstar.

"I've never been much of a screamer and hollerer," he said. "I just think when things are going good, you've got to maintain. And when things are going bad, you've got to maintain."

That is hardly the image one would associate with a basketball superstar, arguably the most complete player in the game this side of Michael Jordan. Yet maintaining his equilibrium on and off the court has enabled Drexler to rise to the top of his profession and earn paychecks that will total $8 million in the final year of his current contract. If his name is not on marquees or his image on billboards, well, he can handle it.

"You have to know who you are," he reflected. "You can't be looking for your identity through newspaper clips or in the bright lights. I've always felt that if things are going to happen, they will. I believe in destiny. If it was meant for me to be the big star, with his name in lights, it would have happened that way. But I don't need it.

"You have to play with the cards that are dealt to you. Money is not

> **"THE ULTIMATE GOAL IS TO WIN A GOLD MEDAL FOR YOUR COUNTRY. I THINK THIS TEAM HAS UNLIMITED POTENTIAL. THERE IS ENORMOUS TALENT AND FLEXIBILITY. I THINK IT WAS A REAL HONOR TO BE CONSIDERED, AND TO BE SELECTED WAS AN EVEN GREATER HONOR. WHEN THEY SAY DREAM TEAM, THAT'S REALLY WHAT THIS IS."**

DREXLER

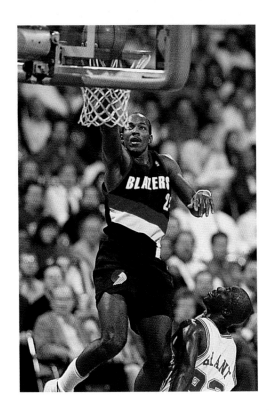

WHEN CLYDE
DREXLER STARTS
TO GLIDE TO THE
BASKET, SOMETIMES
THE ONLY WAY TO
STOP HIM IS TO GRAB
A HANDFUL OF JERSEY.

the reason I play the game, and media exposure isn't a big thing either. Win or lose, I think you have to go on with your life. You have to be happy with yourself."

As for being a big fish in the relatively small though pastoral pond of Portland, Drexler says he's content.

"I've had a great time in Portland. The fans are the best in the NBA. They're behind their team win or lose, and that's a credit to the city of Portland and the state of Oregon. It's a beautiful city. It's like a well-kept secret."

Drexler gives back, both to his hometown of Houston and his new home of Portland, by working at basketball camps and counseling youngsters about the dangers of drug abuse and ways to avoid the lure of the streets—the same streets that claimed an older brother of his, who was shot and killed while trying to rob a Houston drug store.

"To be a role model, you try not to be a hypocrite, that's the No. 1 thing. I think I practice what I preach. I've always had a real strong stand against drugs and alcohol, and I try to relay that same message to the kids.

"Basketball is what gets the kids to camp. But once you get them there, you try to give them a little food for thought."

Clyde Drexler has always been one of the great offensive players in the league, and this year he had one of those magical years. I was particularly impressed with his ability to give up the ball effectively. He's always done it, but never quite like this. His passing of the ball at the right time and the right place really made the Portland Trail Blazers a force in this league.

His game is multifaceted. He can play guard or forward, and he gives us tremendous explosive power at either position. He gives us the flexibility to rotate people into different positions. He can shoot the three-pointer, drive to the basket, post up, or catch the lob and score in the air. On the break, he gets to the basket as well as anyone in the game. He has an ability to slither through traffic, get the ball up on the glass, and score.

He's brought a sense of maturity to the Blazers this year as well. In our case at Detroit, we had to lose to learn how to win an NBA title. Losing helps you understand what winning's all about. There's a maturity factor that has to happen to get to the finals and to win it. Of course, there's a certain amount of luck involved, a lack of injuries, and many other factors. But the Blazers are right there, and Drexler is their key player. He has led them to a place among the NBA's elite teams, a team that could have won the title any of the past three seasons and remains a threat to win it all.

Clyde Drexler has proven he belongs on the Olympic team. If it wasn't for Jordan and Magic, Drexler would have been both the All-Star MVP and the MVP in the league last year.

DREXLER, FLANKED BY TEAMMATES BUCK WILLIAMS (LEFT) AND JEROME KERSEY (RIGHT), LED THE PORTLAND TRAIL BLAZERS TO THE NBA FINALS IN 1990 AND AGAIN IN 1992.

CLYDE "THE GLIDE" DREXLER

Guard

Portland Trail Blazers

6-7, 222, 30 years old

Birthdate: June 22, 1962

High School: Sterling, Houston, Texas

College: Houston

• Nine-year NBA veteran

• Six-time NBA All-Star

• All-NBA First Team once (1992), Second Team twice (1988 and 1991), Third Team once (1990).

• Holds NBA Playoff record for most points in an overtime period, 13 (April 29, 1992 vs. LA Lakers).

• Ranked fourth in NBA in scoring in 1992 at 25.0 points per game.

• Led Portland Trail Blazers to NBA Finals twice (1990 and 1992).

• Led Portland Trail Blazers in scoring five straight seasons (1988 through 1992).

• NBA career averages: 21.0 points, 6.1 rebounds, 5.8 assists.

"*EVERYTHING YOU HEAR me say is basically what I learned from my parents," said Patrick Ewing, the All-Star center of the New York Knicks who was born in Jamaica and moved to Cambridge, Massachusetts, with his parents when he was 12 years old. "They both told me to work hard."*

Hard work has paid off for Ewing, who has pursued what he felt was important—whether it was academics or athletics—with dogged determination, a purposefulness that would mark his entire basketball career from high school to the NBA.

"He was the same then as he is now," observed Mike Jarvis, Ewing's coach at Cambridge Rindge & Latin High School and now the coach at George Washington University. "He was a hard worker, and if he didn't know something, he'd ask you a thousand times until he got it right. He wasn't always a great player. He went through times where he was clumsy and awkward. We had to tell him to be tall, walk tall, be proud."

Ewing's solid work ethic, combined with his physical skills, enabled him to become one of the country's most highly recruited high school players. He chose to attend Georgetown, in part because he saw a role model in Hoyas Coach John Thompson, and the two remain close.

"He's the best," Ewing said of Thompson, who coached the 1988 U.S. Olympic team. "He's a great person. He taught me a lot about basketball and about life. I grew a lot in the four years I was there."

"IT'S AN HONOR TO BE SELECTED. I ALREADY PLAYED WITH MICHAEL JORDAN ON THE '84 TEAM. THIS WILL BE ANOTHER GREAT EXPERIENCE, PLAYING WITH HIM AGAIN AND ALL THE OTHER NBA STARS. THE '92 TEAM IS DEFINITELY A BETTER TEAM THAN THE '84 TEAM. IT WILL BE A GREAT HONOR TO PLAY FOR THE UNITED STATES AGAIN."

EWING

In those four years, Ewing led the Hoyas to one NCAA championship and two more NCAA finals. He was the college Player of the Year and won a gold medal with the U.S. Olympic team in Los Angeles in 1984. Reknowned for his shotblocking and his tenacity, he was considered a "franchise" player when he was selected by the New York Knicks, winners of the first-ever NBA Draft Lottery in 1985. There was tremendous pressure on Ewing when he turned pro, and even though he won Rookie of the Year, some considered him a disappointment because the Knicks did not become instant winners.

"There's pressure in everything," he said. "I don't worry about it. I just play basketball."

And play it well. Ewing has become a perennial All-Star, scoring far more than he did in college while also ranking among the NBA leaders in rebounding and shotblocking.

FROM THE NCAA TO THE NBA, PATRICK EWING HAS BEEN ONE OF BASKETBALL'S DOMINANT BIG MEN FOR THE PAST DECADE.

"I still am a defensive-minded player," the 7-footer maintained. "I still want to play defense and try to stop people—that's the only way you can win in this league or any league. You've got to be able to stop

people. But you've also got to be capable of scoring."

While the Knicks have yet to win an NBA title with Ewing, he has become the mainstay of the franchise, the hub around which the team revolves. And he is focused on winning.

"All the scoring titles and all the rebounding titles don't make a difference if you're losing," he said. "They all remember the winners. All that matters to me is when the game is over and I look up at the scoreboard and we're the winning team. That's it—that's the bottom line."

We play against Patrick Ewing all the time and I've always had great respect for his ability, but you never really know about a player until you're directly involved with him. The year I coached in the NBA All-Star Game, I thought that day he was the MVP. He controlled the lane, and I was stunned by the intensity with which he played. I've said all along, you never know a player until you coach him, even if you only coach him for one game.

My opinion of Ewing went sky-high because of that competitiveness, that toughness, that physical quality he gives you in the lane. He's a great shooter, not a dominant rebounder but still good, an excellent shotblocker. And he loves to win.

With Ewing and Robinson, we can really do some things. They're both great shotblockers who can really control the lane. You can play them together because they're both very mobile. Defensively, I don't think you have to double-team—I say play straight up and make the other team beat you over the top. That way we can control the three-point line, which is vital in international play.

Our coaching staff must answer intriguing questions. Who do you start? Who do you bring off the bench? Can you play these two centers together? What combinations will work best? We're going to be staying up late plenty of nights, I can tell you. But with great centers like Ewing and Robinson, these are problems coaches love to face.

PATRICK ALOYSIUS EWING

Center

New York Knicks

7-0, 240, 30 years old

Birthdate: August 5, 1962

High School: Cambridge
Rindge & Latin, Mass.

College: Georgetown

• Seven-year NBA veteran

• Six-time NBA All-Star

• All-NBA First Team once
(1990), Second Team four
times (1988, 1989, 1991
and 1992).

• NBA All-Rookie Team, 1986.

• Led Georgetown to NCAA
championship in 1984 and
runnerup in 1985.

• Most Outstanding Player
of NCAA tournament, 1984.

• Led New York Knicks in
scoring and blocked shots
in each of his seven NBA
seasons (1986 through
1992).

• NBA career averages:
23.6 points, 9.9 rebounds,
3.09 blocks.

"*I* ALWAYS DREAMED *of being the hero of the game," mused Magic Johnson. "The game would be tied, they would call my play, and I would make the shot at the buzzer. And just as I hit it, I always woke up. It was a dream."*

As a youngster growing up in Lansing, Michigan, Earvin Johnson, Jr., displayed both a passionate commitment to the game of basketball and a work ethic he inherited from his parents, Earvin, Sr., and Christine. "I loved the game so much," he recalled, "I would just go out there and play all day and all night. Whether I was carrying groceries, or running an errand for my mom or dad, I always had one hand free to dribble that basketball."

His sister, Evelyn, vouches for that. "We'd have four or five feet of snow on the ground, and he'd get up early, go shovel off the court, and shoot," she said.

Johnson's talent for the game was evident early, and his reputation preceded him to Everett High School. "I told all my friends that I had a kid coming in here who would make them forget about any other basketball player in the area, or maybe any other player they ever saw," said George Fox, Magic's high school coach. "We knew we had something special. He was a phenomenal player."

It was in high school that Johnson picked up the nickname "Magic." Sports writer Fred Stabley was covering a game for the Lansing State Journal *and felt the hoop prodigy needed a proper moniker.*

Johnson went on to become perhaps the ultimate basketball winner.

"I'M HAPPY TO BE SELECTED AND TO HAVE THE OPPOR-TUNITY TO PLAY WITH OTHER GREAT, GREAT BASKETBALL PLAYERS. I WOULDN'T MISS THE OLYMPICS FOR ANYTHING. I'M LOOKING FORWARD TO BRINGING HOME THE GOLD."

JOHNSON

He led Everett to the 1977 Michigan state high school championship, Michigan State to the 1979 NCAA championship, and the Los Angeles Lakers to NBA titles in 1980, 1982, 1985, 1987, and 1988. His Lakers were acclaimed as the NBA's "Team of the Decade," and he was named as the game's "Player of the Decade."

"I only play to win, that's it," he said. "I love to win. I'll do whatever it takes to win."

And do it with style and charisma. Johnson's smile, as much as his skill in running his team's "Showtime" offense, made the Lakers the hot ticket in Los Angeles. Actors, film producers, record industry executives, and assorted other moguls vied to see and be seen courtside at the Forum, to bask in the warm glow of Magic's smile.

Magic revolutionized his position, combining point guard skills with a power forward's body. His trademark became the no-look pass, where he would race downcourt as the middle man in a fast break, look off the defender, and quickly whip a pass to an open teammate on the other side of the floor.

"My eyes get so big when I'm coming down the court, I don't know what I'm going to do," he said. "I'm shakin', I'm bakin', that's when I'm at my best."

"I don't think there will ever be another 6-9 point guard who smiles while he humiliates you," observed long-time Lakers teammate James Worthy, a frequent beneficiary of Johnson's passes.

Magic's passion for the game breathed new life into the Los Angeles Lakers and their stalwart center, Kareem Abdul-Jabbar. His performance in Game 6 of the 1980 NBA Finals, when as a 20-year-old rookie he filled in for the injured Abdul-Jabbar at center and responded with 42 points, 15 rebounds, and 7 assists as the Lakers wrapped up the title against the Philadelphia 76ers, is perhaps the greatest single-game effort in NBA playoff history.

WHEN MAGIC JOHNSON MET MICHAEL JORDAN IN THE 1991 NBA FINALS, IT WAS A MATCHUP OF TWO OF THE NBA'S ALL-TIME GREAT GUARDS.

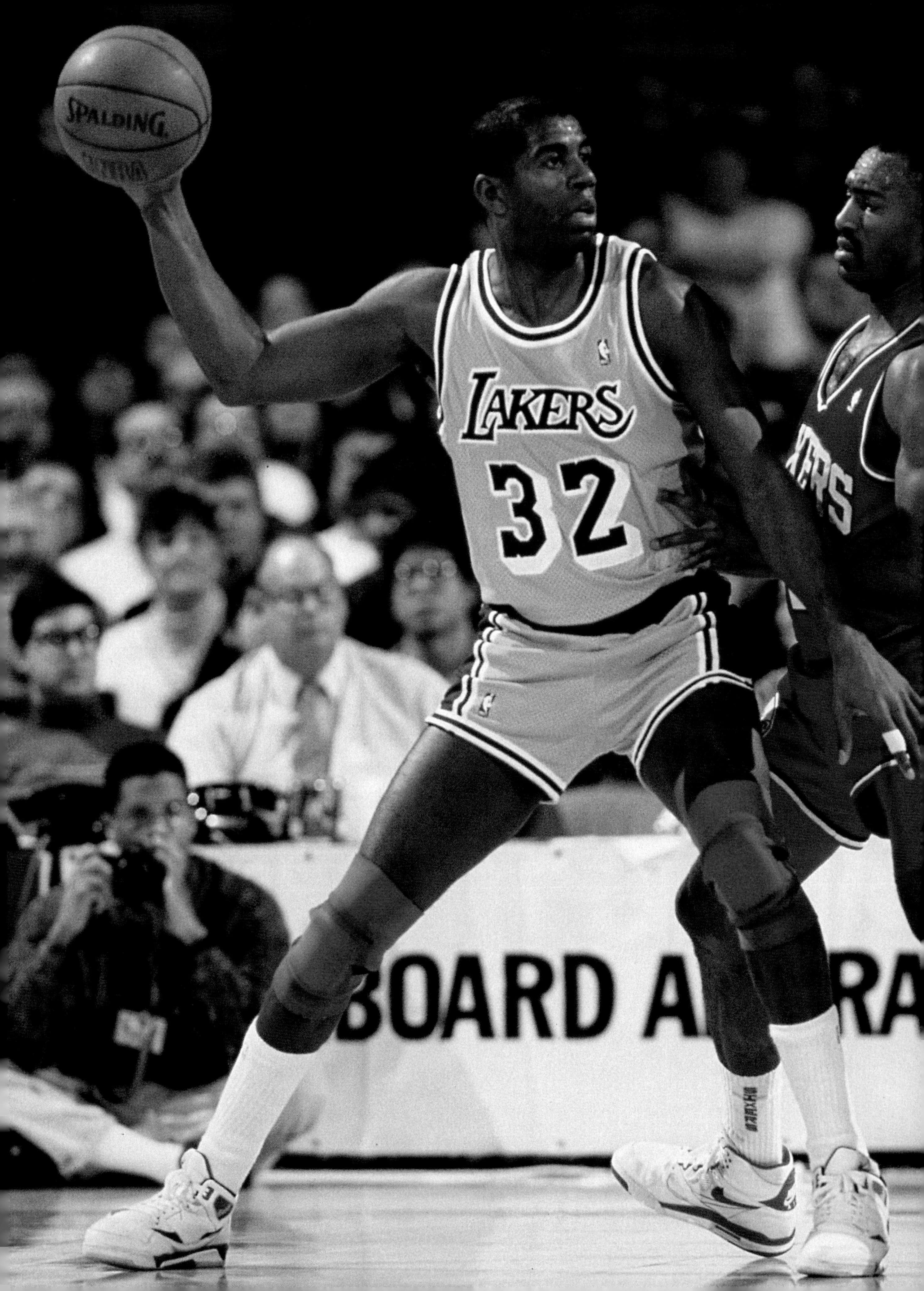
SPALDING
LAKERS
32
BOARD

"Every shot was a big shot, every rebound a big rebound, every assist a big assist," said Johnson. "I think I had lived for a moment like this, and finally I was caught up in it."

This time, it was not a dream.

When you talk about Magic, you talk about winning. He's a big-time winner, everywhere he's been. He's in the Bird mold in that he makes everybody he plays with a basket or two better per game. His general enthusiasm for the game and his upbeat personality make him the charismatic individual that he is.

He is unique in having point guard skills yet standing 6-9. That lets him make passes nobody else can make, since he has better passing angles because of his height.

He's a great player, don't get me wrong, but athletically, I don't think he's in the category of a Jordan in terms of quickness of movement, overall agility, and so forth. But here's a guy who has dedicated himself to making the most of his abilities.

I remember scouting him when he was a freshman in college. I was working for the 76ers at the time, and we had to fill out a card after we got back describing the player we were scouting. I wrote, "I think he drove the bus, I think he flew the plane. No questions." He was that good, as a freshman.

And he's only gotten better, because of his tremendous dedication to developing new phases of his game. That separates the good players from the great players—the level of dedication to working on your game. Magic knew he'd be going to the foul line a lot, so he became a 90 percent free-throw shooter. He knew defenders were going to lay off him to keep him from driving to the basket, so he developed a three-point shot.

It's been unbelieveable the way the NBA has taken off since Magic and Bird came into the league. Their charisma, the team aspect of the way they play, their devotion to winning—all those things add up to entertainment for the public.

Magic is always a gentleman. He always has time for people.

ALWAYS ABLE TO RELATE TO THOSE LESS FORTUNATE THAN HIMSELF, JOHNSON DEVOTES CONSIDERABLE TIME, EFFORT, AND MONEY TO CHARITY WORK.

It's a joy for him to be playing; it isn't like it's a job. When you have players who love to play and show it, then the public identifies with them.

I've always enjoyed competing against Magic Johnson and am eagerly anticipating the chance to coach him. I can see him emerging as the on-court leader of this team, because he has the respect of everyone in the league.

WITH HIS TRADE-MARK SMILE ALWAYS EVIDENT, THE MAGIC MAN'S JOY IN PLAYING THE GAME IS CLEAR TO ALL.

EARVIN "MAGIC" JOHNSON, JR.

Guard

Los Angeles Lakers

6-9, 225, 33 years old

Birthdate: August 14, 1959

High School: Everett, Lansing, Michigan

College: Michigan State

• 13-year NBA veteran

• 12-time NBA All-Star

• Three-time NBA Most Valuable Player (1987, 1989 and 1990).

• Three-time NBA Finals Most Valuable Player (1980, 1982, 1987).

• Two-time NBA All-Star Game Most Valubale Player (1990 and 1992).

• Led Los Angeles Lakers to five NBA World Championships (1980, 1982, 1985, 1987 and 1988).

• NBA's all-time leader in assists in regular season, playoff and All-Star competition.

• Led NBA in assists four times (1983, 1984, 1986 and 1987), steals twice (1981 and 1982) and free throw pecentage once (1989)

• NBA career averages: 19.7 points, 7.3 rebounds, 10.6 assists.

WITH HIS RARE COMBINATION of style and substance, grit and grace, Michael Jordan has captured the imagination of sports fans and non–sports fans alike. He is the dominant player in the NBA, winner of the league scoring championship each of the last six years and the NBA's Most Valuable Player in 1988, 1991, and 1992. "Air" Jordan is the most popular athlete in the world, the idol of millions, young and old, and an inspiration to anyone who ever was judged not good enough to play for his 10th-grade team.

That's what happened to Jordan during his sophomore year at Laney High School in Wilmington, North Carolina. Basketball coach Fred Lynch cut him during varsity tryouts, thus doing Jordan perhaps the biggest favor of his life.

"Every time I play, I feel like I've got something to prove," Jordan says, more than a decade later. "Getting cut in high school has a lot to do with that. I was really surprised and embarrassed when the coach cut me. That's when I started to take the game seriously. I know it's years later, but I still refuse to take anything for granted. I get up for every game. I need that kind of intensity. That's what keeps me going.

"I love the game. To me, playing basketball has never been a job. Just because I'm getting paid doesn't make it a job. I couldn't put myself on the line the way I do, night after night, if it was just a job. I love to compete and I hate to lose. I take it very personally."

Jordan's competitiveness was nurtured in one-on-one games against

"THE BIGGEST KEY TO OUR TEAM'S SUCCESS IS BEING ABLE TO PLAY TOGETHER. I'M HAPPY TO BE A PART OF THIS TEAM AND NOT HAVE TO SCORE 30 OR 40 POINTS A GAME. WE KNOW OUR REPUTATION WILL PRECEDE US, SO WE WANT TO TAKE IT RIGHT AT THE FOREIGN TEAMS. WE'RE HERE TO REGAIN THE PRIDE AND DIGNITY OF U.S. BASKETBALL. WE WANT PEOPLE TO REMEMBER THAT THIS IS WHERE THE GAME WAS CREATED."

JORDAN

*older brother Larry, who preceded Michael as a star guard at Laney
High School and whom Michael idolized. When Michael, after
growing four inches in one year, finally made the Laney varsity during
his junior year, he took the number 23 because it was about half his
brother's number 45.*

*He's frequently asked what it felt like to dunk the ball for the first
time. "I always dreamed about dunking the ball and making
spectacular moves," he said. "I wanted to dunk so badly that I started
practicing on 8- and 9-foot rims. By the time I got into the 11th grade,
I could dunk pretty easily on a 10-foot rim. The first time I attempted
a 10-foot dunk, I barely did it. I thought I was going to lay it up, but I
just turned it over. It was kind of a baby dunk, but it was still a dunk.
Man, did I feel great!"*

Michael's talents are almost indescribable. He has a small
forward's body and the quickness of a guard. He has perhaps the
most athletic quickness of anyone who has ever played in the
NBA. He's got a complete offensive game—great moves to the
basket, incredible leaping ability, and the touch of the best
shooters from up to three-point range.

Then you add what he's capable of doing defensively, both
individually and within the team defense, and you have the
complete package. One reason the Chicago Bulls are so tough is
that on just about every team, the 2 guard is one of the biggest
scorers, and Jordan practically eliminates that guy because he's
so good defensively. So all of a sudden your team goes from
scoring 101 points to 91 points or less, and you've got a major
offensive problem.

Then there are the intangibles—the competitiveness, wanting
to win every time out. There are a lot of guys who have talent—
they don't have Michael Jordan's talent, but they have talent—
but they don't want to win badly enough, and so they give in to
fatigue. He never gives in to fatigue, which is quite a gift.

And he's a driving force on his team, a leader. Athletic

WHEN MICHAEL
JORDAN'S LONG-TIME
DREAM OF WINNING
AN NBA WORLD
CHAMPIONSHIP
WAS REALIZED IN
1991, HE BROKE
DOWN IN TEARS.

basketball skills aren't enough to win in our league. So much of winning is mental. You have to have mental toughness along with the skills. I'm not sure that the rest of the Chicago players would reach the level that they have without Jordan as the driving force, motivating them on a day-to-day basis.

All those things make him easily one of the greatest players ever to play the game.

JORDAN IS AN AVID COMPETITOR, WHETHER IT'S ON THE BASKETBALL COURT OR THE GOLF LINKS. HE FIRST EARNED OLYMPIC GOLD IN 1984.

THE SIGHT OF JORDAN SOARING TO THE BASKET, AHEAD OF THE
FIELD, FOR ONE OF HIS RIM-RATTLING DUNKS ALWAYS BRINGS
THE CROWD TO ITS FEET.

MICHAEL "AIR" JORDAN

Guard

Chicago Bulls

6-6, 198, 29 years old

Birthdate: February 17, 1963

High School: Laney, Wilmington, North Carolina

College: North Carolina

• Eight-year NBA veteran.

• Eight-year NBA All-Star.

• Three-time NBA Most Valuable Player (1988, 1991, 1992).

• Two-time NBA Finals Most Valuable Player (1991 and 1992).

• NBA All-Star Game Most Valuable Player, 1988.

• NBA all-time leader in scoring average for regular season (32.3), playoffs (34.6) and All-Star (21.0).

• Led NBA in scoring six straight seasons (1987 through 1992).

• NBA Defensive Player of the Year, 1988.

• Two-time winner of Schick Award for overall contributions to team's success (1985 and 1989).

• NBA career averages: 32.3 points, 6.3 rebounds, 6.0 assists

BONNIE LAETTNER LIKED Marlon Brando so much, she named her second son Christian after the characters Brando played in Mutiny on the Bounty *and* The Young Lions. *This despite the fact that she already had named her first son Christopher.*

Perhaps even then she knew that having an older sibling with a similar name would not hamper Christian in any way.

Few college athletes in recent years have aroused such strong feelings as Laettner, the key figure on Duke University's back-to-back NCAA title teams in 1991 and 1992 and the lone collegian on the USA Basketball team.

Sports Illustrated *headlined him as "pivotman and paradox: agile giant, trash-talking preppy, angelic bruiser."*

He's been named Man of the Year—not by Time Magazine *but by the* Harvard Lampoon, *a magazine which once gave it's Man of the Year award to Brooke Shields.*

His admirers see Laettner as Jack Armstrong for the 1990s, the All-American boy but with a razor edge, intelligent and articulate, blue-eyed and handsome enough to attract the attention of GQ and People *magazines, yet sufficiently self-assured to speak his mind. His detractors see Laettner as cocky rather than confident, brash rather than bold, the kind of player who is equally likely to jaw with teammates as opponents.*

Laettner has done little, if anything, to dispel the jumbled image that has been projected of him. He clearly enjoys the media attention.

"IT WILL BE FUN, PLAYING WITH JORDAN AND BIRD AND THOSE GUYS. I'M SURE I WON'T PLAY MUCH ON THAT TEAM, BUT IT WILL BE A GREAT EXPERIENCE FOR PLAYING IN THE NBA. JUST BEING IN THE OLYMPICS WILL BE GREAT."

LAETTNER

WITH COVER-BOY LOOKS AND ATHLETIC SKILLS TO MATCH, CHRISTIAN LAETTNER GAINED NATIONAL PROMINENCE AT DUKE.

"They made a celebrity out of me, and I like that," he said. "And I don't think it's going to hurt me. People like Bo Jackson or Muhammad Ali, there was so much more to them than their sport. They were athletes who had more than just athletics, and I like that a lot.

"Of course I enjoy the notoriety. If I didn't want to be in this situation, I wouldn't play basketball."

But play basketball he does, and very well. He has the size and strength to mix it up under the basket and the deft shooting touch and ball-handling skills to be effective from long range. He can play in the pivot or facing the basket, inside or outside, and is at his best when the game is on the line, as evidenced by his two free throws with 12 seconds left that gave Duke a 79–77 decision over UNLV in the 1991 NCAA title game and his turnaround buzzer-beater against Kentucky in the 1992 East Regional final. He is the only man to start in four NCAA Final Fours and the leading scorer in the history of the NCAA tournament with 407 points in four years.

"Christian has this hunger for competition that I've never seen in anybody else," said Duke Coach (and USAB assistant) Mike Krzyzewski. "He's never afraid to make the play, be it a shot, rebound, pass, block, whatever. He wants to be there when the game is decided.

"You've heard of guys who burn to win? This guy's got a forest fire inside him."

Like all basketball fans, I've watched Christian Laettner develop into an outstanding player and a real winner.

I sincerely think that this year we had a great collegiate crew that could have played very well in the Olympic Games. Take Christian Laettner, Shaquille O'Neal, Alonzo Mourning, Jim Jackson, Harold Miner for openers—these are five outstanding players. All were capable of playing on the USAB team.

Christian's strengths are his overall game, his versatility, his toughness, and his winning record. Here's a guy who brought Duke to the Final Four in each of his four years, and two years they won it all. There has to be something that brings a player or a team to that level year in and year out. I think the selection committee was impressed by his winning record, as well as his experience in international competition.

He has great tools and also a mental toughness. I'm sure the committee looked at his maturity and said, "Here's a guy who can handle going with 11 NBA players." And that will not be an easy chore! I loved Charles Barkley's statement that Laettner is going to be the strongest rookie in the NBA because he's going to be carting our luggage around all summer! Laettner will also have the toughest skin, because I'm sure he's going to get his share of verbal abuse. But I'm confident they'll take him into the fold and he will hold his own. He's a good enough player to be a factor and to be a part of this group.

LAETTNER WAS A KEY FIGURE ON DUKE COACH MIKE KRZYZEWSKI'S TWO NCAA CHAMPION- SHIP TEAMS.

CHRISTIAN DONALD LAETTNER

Forward/Center

Minnesota Timberwolves

6-11, 235, 23 years old

Birthdate: August 17, 1969

High School: Nichols School, Buffalo, New York.

College: Duke

• Entering first NBA season.

• Selected on first round of 1992 NBA Draft, third pick overall.

• Led Duke to consecutive NCAA championships (1991 and 1992).

• Named Most Outstanding Player of NCAA tournament, 1992.

• Only player ever to start in four NCAA Final Fours (1989 through 1992).

• Holds NCAA tournament records for points (407), games (23) free throws made (142) and attempted (167) and is tied for record in steals (32).

• Holds NCAA record for most games played (148).

• Career averages (at Duke): 16.6 points, 7.8 rebounds, 1.8 assists.

KARL MALONE GREW UP *in rural northwestern Louisiana, far from the spotlight of big-time athletics, and shot his first basketball through a homemade hoop.*

"We did everything the old-fashioned way," said Malone. "We'd get an old bicycle tire, knock the spokes out of it and put haywire on it. That was our basket. Then we'd go out and cut down an old oak tree—we never knew whose property we were on—and we'd make our backboard. And we'd play on dirt, red clay that got all over our shoes, our clothes, everything."

Malone quickly became hooked on basketball, but not on books. The turning point came when he got to Louisiana Tech for his freshman year and learned he was ineligible to play basketball because his grade point average wasn't high enough.

"I had let my family down," he recalled. "I had let Karl Malone down. I was at the point where I said, 'Karl, are you going to be a loser the rest of your life, or are you going to do something positive with yourself? You can either go to college or sit at home and be what everybody expects you to be, which is nothing.'"

Malone concentrated on his studies as a freshman, got his GPA up, and then starred for three seasons at Tech, where he earned the nickname "the Mailman" because he always delivered. He wept upon being selected by the Utah Jazz in the first round of the NBA Draft in 1985, recognizing the enormous odds he had overcome to make it to the NBA. But he didn't stop there.

"I'M HONORED AND DELIGHTED TO GO. ANY TIME YOU HAVE THE OPPORTUNITY TO REPRESENT YOUR COUNTRY, IT'S AN HONOR. IF I CAN SERVE MY COUNTRY IN ANY WAY, I'M GLAD TO DO IT. WE'RE GOING TO BRING BACK THE GOLD."

MALONE

"I said, 'Kid in a candy store, you got that now. OK, what do you really want? Do you want to be an OK basketball player? Or do you want to be a great one?' I wanted to be a great one."

So Malone set out to maximize his assets. He pumped iron and sculpted his 6-9, 256-pound physique, building his strength and endurance. He quickly became the dominant player at his position, power forward, an NBA All-Star each of the last five years.

"I don't think there's ever been anybody chiseled like Karl Malone, who can do what he does," said New York Knicks Coach Pat Riley. Added Los Angeles Lakers forward James Worthy, "Every play, every rebound, you are going to have to go harder than you would go against anybody else in the league."

"His ability to score inside and outside is pretty well noted," said Jazz and 1992 Olympic teammate John Stockton, "but there's also his ability to run the floor. On the fast break, I've watched a hundred times where he gets a rebound, outlets it to me, and then beats me down to the other end of the court to get an open lay-up. Over the course of the game, he'll wear you down."

A POWERFUL FORCE UNDER THE BASKET, KARL "THE MAILMAN" MALONE HAS HELPED THE UTAH JAZZ BECOME AN NBA TITLE CONTENDER.

Karl is the prototype power forward. He may be the single strongest person in the league. His strength is going to be important, because from what I've seen of international play, when the clock winds down, often the whistles stop. You need guys who can power the ball to the basket, and he and Barkley are two big, strong guys who can do that.

He's an All-Star performer who's capable of getting from 25 to 40 points every night. He's as fast a big man as I've ever seen for his physical equipment, and he has surprisingly fine shooting touch for a man of his strength. He's a great offensive player, a very physical player, and a great guy to have on the team.

I don't know who sold him on the idea of building himself up the way he has, but it certainly was a great idea because that strength has made him what he is. It's almost impossible to stop him from getting off his shot because of his strength.

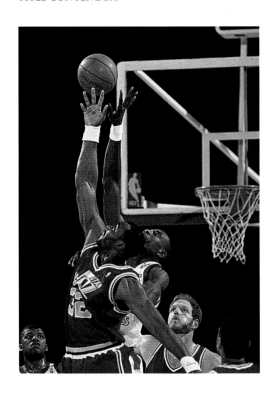

That kind of dedication says a lot about Karl Malone. Many guys come into the league and want to rely just on their basketball ability. They don't want to do the hard work that goes into building a body like Karl Malone's. He's got the kind of dedication that makes a person great.

MALONE'S CHISELED
BODY SPEAKS
VOLUMES ABOUT
HIS DEDICATION
AND WORK ETHIC.

KARL
"THE MAILMAN"
MALONE

Forward

Utah Jazz

6-9, 256, 29 years old
Birthdate: July 24, 1963
High School: Summerfield,
Louisiana
College: Louisiana Tech
• Seven-year NBA veteran.
• Five-time NBA All-Star.
• All-Star Game Most
Valuable Player, 1989.
• All-NBA First Team four
straight seasons (1989
through 1992), Second
Team once (1988).
• NBA All-Rookie Team,
1986.
• Jazz' all-time leading scorer
with 14,770 points.
• Has ranked second in
NBA in scoring four straight
seasons (1989 through
1992).
• Has led Jazz in scoring
six straight seasons (1987
through 1992).
• Became ninth player in
NBA history to average over
30 points (31.0) and 10
rebounds (11.1) in 1990.
• NBA career averages:
25.9 points, 10.9 rebounds,
2.7 assists.

CHRIS MULLIN IS A GYM RAT. You never know when you will find him in a gym, shooting hoops, working on his game.

When he was at Xaverian High School in Brooklyn, he made it easier on everyone by getting a key to the school gym from a custodian, so he wouldn't have to wake anyone up for one of his after-hours shoot-arounds. He did the same thing at St. John's, where he earned All-America honors, and with the Golden State Warriors, where he has become an NBA All-Star and the club's leading scorer for five consecutive seasons.

"Chris is always in great condition and has tremendous stamina," said Don Nelson, the Warriors' coach and general manager. "He's always working on his body and his game. He can play 48 minutes one night and show no effects the following day."

For Mullin, a recovering alcoholic, working out is an important part of his treatment.

"We've already determined that I'm an addictive personality," he once reflected, while pedaling a stationary bicycle. "Now, every day I come to practice, I'm so happy. I remember it wasn't always like this. All the good things that have happened to me have happened for a reason, and that's because I quit drinking. I know that if that doesn't happen, nothing else does."

For inspiration he turns to the memory of his father, Rod, another recovering alcoholic, who died of bone cancer two summers ago.

"BEING SELECTED FOR THE USA BASKETBALL TEAM IS MIND-BOGGLING. I HAVE TO STEP BACK AND ENJOY IT, OTHERWISE IT CAN BE INTIMIDATING. THE MAIN REASON EVERYONE AGREED TO PLAY WAS TO WIN. WHATEVER IT TAKES, IT'S SOMETHING WE ALL WANT TO DO."

MULLIN

"The last five minutes when he was still with us, I was in there crying," Mullin said, recalling his final hospital visit. "I was sweating, and he was saying, 'What, did you just finish working out? What's wrong?' Five minutes later he just stopped breathing, nice and peaceful, just like that.

"He treated everyone the same. He had time for everyone, no matter who you were or what your background. He was always so positive. I can still feel my father's presence. I kind of still live my life as if he's around, which he is to me. He's not that far from me at all."

As a youngster, basketball wasn't Mullin's only sport—he showed talent in baseball and swimming as well. However, swimming laps or shagging flies never appealed to Mullin the way shooting hoops did, so he devoted himself to basketball.

"I wouldn't go play baseball or swim on my own, but basketball was different," recalled Mullin. "When I had spare time, I always played basketball. I'd watch basketball on TV, and whoever had a good day, that's who I'd be. I'd watch the game and go right into my backyard and play, imitating Earl Monroe, Walt Frazier, Pistol Pete Maravich, John Havlicek, whoever was on that day."

Growing up in Brooklyn, then going on to college in Queens, Mullin became well-known on the blacktop playgrounds of New York. "I played up in the Bronx, all over the city, in the worst neighborhoods," said Mullin. "And not only did I get a sense of the game, I got acceptance. They would leave me alone because I could play. When I first started going into some neighborhoods, I'd have to ask guys on the team to walk me from the court to the train station because I wasn't safe. By the time I was a senior in high school, I was fine. All the fellas in the neighborhoods knew me."

Now sports fans all around the world know Chris Mullin, two-time U.S. Olympian and NBA All-Star, the man with the drill sergeant crew cut and the big-time game.

Chris was an easy choice for the selection committee. He's a fabulous offensive player, a great three-point shooter, great at

CHRIS MULLIN, WHO LED ST. JOHN'S TO FOUR NCAA TOURNEY BERTHS, SAYS HE FAVORS A CREW CUT BECAUSE IT'S VIRTUALLY MAINTENANCE FREE.

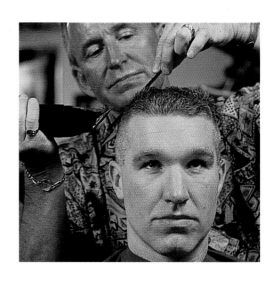

MULLIN HAS BECOME
THE MAINSTAY
OF THE GOLDEN
STATE WARRIORS,
ANNUALLY RANKING
AMONG THE NBA'S
TOP SCORERS.

getting into the lane, an excellent passer. He's a guy who really, really knows how to play. He can defend adequately. He can guard the three-point line, and he's a silent killer when it comes to steals—he has a way of coming from behind and getting steals before you know it.

He's obviously one of the main reasons for Golden State's success. He's an All-Star performer who does so many things well. His versatility is a major plus, too. He can play guard or forward and gives us valuable protection in case of injury at either position, since once we get to Barcelona we can't change our roster.

Another thing about Chris is that he really knows how to play the game of basketball—and wants to play. That's an ingredient you have to like as a coach, especially with a team of stars like the Olympic team. Chris will take any role you give him and be happy with it. He can be a starter, a sixth man, an eighth man, whatever, as long as he's playing ball.

He's a basketball junkie who really loves to play. As a kid, he used to travel all over New York, always looking for the toughest challenge, whether it was the playgrounds of Harlem or wherever. That certainly helped his game.

CHRISTOPHER PAUL MULLIN

Forward/Guard

Golden State Warriors

6-7, 215, 29 years old

Birthdate: July 30, 1963

High School: Xaverian, Brooklyn, New York

College: St. John's

• Seven-year NBA veteran.

• Four-time NBA All-Star.

• All-NBA First Team, 1992; Second Team twice (1989, 1991); Third Team, 1990.

• Has led Warriors in scoring for five straight seasons (1988 through 1992).

• Has led NBA in minutes played for two straight seasons (1991 and 1992).

• Career free-throw percentage of .874 ranks eighth in all-time NBA history and third among active players.

• Led St. John's to four NCAA tournament berth, including Final Four in 1985.

• NBA career averages: 22.2 points, 4.5 rebounds, 3.9 assists

SOME PLAYERS COME INTO THE NBA as full-blown stars, household names thanks to having played in big-time college programs before national television audiences. Scottie Pippen came into the NBA after having played college ball at the University of Central Arkansas, and about the only household in which he was a name was the Pippen residence in tiny Hamburg, Arkansas (population 3,394).

Basketball did not come easily for Pippen, the youngest of 12 children. Even at Hamburg High School he didn't make the starting five until his senior year, and when his coach got him a grant to attend Central Arkansas, Pippen's original intent was to serve as the team's equipment manager.

"I wasn't really that interested in playing," recalled Pippen. "I had gone through some hard times not playing in high school, but my coach had it in his mind that basketball was the way I would get an education."

He was given a chance to try out and won a spot on the playing roster as a freshman. By the following year he had grown to 6-5 and blossomed into the best player on the team. Pippen improved rapidly and averaged 23.6 points, 10 rebounds, and 4.3 assists per game as a senior; shooting a phenomenal 58 percent from three-point range. By then, word was out on the NBA scouting grapevine about the lean, lanky youngster from Central Arkansas.

"PLAYING ON THE OLYMPIC TEAM IS A GREAT OPPORTUNITY FOR ME. I GOT THE CALL ASKING IF I'D PLAY AND MY ANSWER WAS A STRAIGHT-OUT YES. I DIDN'T HAVE ANY SECOND THOUGHTS ABOUT PLAYING WITH PEOPLE WHO I HAD ALWAYS LOOKED UP TO AS A KID."

PIPPEN

WHILE MICHAEL JORDAN MAY GARNER THE HEADLINES, BULLS TEAMMATE SCOTTIE PIPPEN HAS EMERGED AS ONE OF THE NBA'S FINEST ALL-AROUND PLAYERS.

"We wanted to try to sneak him past people, but you can't hide a guy with that kind of ability," said Billy McKinney, formerly the Chicago Bulls' director of player personnel. So the Bulls swung a deal with Seattle, which had a higher position in the 1988 NBA Draft, and landed the player who would become the perfect complement to Michael Jordan.

Pippen has improved steadily in his five years in the NBA, boosting his scoring, rebounding, and assist totals every year to the point where he is now recognized as one of the sport's superstars.

"Playing with a guy like Michael, you have to take a lot of pride in what you're doing," reflected Pippen. "You don't want to fall that far behind. Even though you know you have to take a back seat to him, you always want to be a competitive player."

Scottie is a late bloomer who has reached the status of superstar. This is a guy who has just moved up, up, up the ladder in our league.

Early on he showed he had the athletic skills, but I'm not sure he had the confidence. I think by playing with Jordan, the confidence rubbed off on him. It also brought out his competitiveness—he had to show, every night, that he could hold his own with the best.

He always had great quickness and agility, but over the past few years he's developed to the point where he's now a great shooter, too. He has good size and can play multiple positions—really, all positions except center. He's a good rebounder and shot-blocker and an outstanding defensive player.

Pippen and Jordan being probably two of the top five defensive players in the league makes Chicago so tough. They have the ability to retreat deep into the defense and recover better than anybody else in the league. That makes them so dangerous in terms of making steals.

One of the greatest assets for the Olympic team is Pippen's versatility, his ability to play multiple positions and defend against virtually anyone—Toni Kukoc, Oscar Schmidt, anyone.

He's a big-time stopper. He can defend the ball, he can defend off the ball, and he can defend the three-point line, which is going to be crucial in international competition. His outstanding defense against Magic Johnson was perhaps the key to the Bulls' victory in the 1991 NBA Finals. When the coaching staff moved him against Magic, that completely changed the complexion of the series. He found a way to take Magic pretty much out of the game, and that really crippled the Lakers.

He truly has surfaced as one of the great players in the game.

PIPPEN, WHO DIDN'T MAKE HIS HIGH SCHOOL'S STARTING LINEUP UNTIL HIS SENIOR YEAR, IS A CLASSIC LATE BLOOMER WHO CONTINUES TO IMPROVE EACH SEASON.

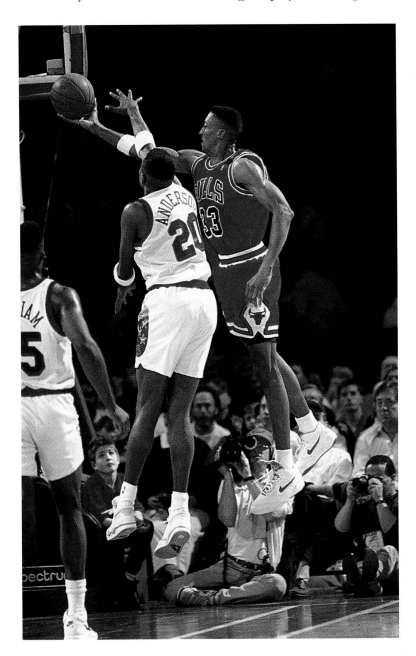

SCOTTIE PIPPEN

Forward/Guard

Chicago Bulls

6-7, 210, 27 years old

Birthdate: September 25, 1965

High School: Hamburg, Arkansas

College: Central Arkansas

• Five-year NBA veteran.

• Two-time NBA All-Star.

• All-NBA Second Team, 1992.

• NBA All-Defensive First Team, 1992; All-Defensive Second Team, 1991.

• Helped lead Chicago Bulls to two straight NBA Championships (1991-92).

• Has led Bulls in assists two straight seasons (1991 and 1992).

• Ranked third in NBA in steals (2.57) in 1990 and fifth (2.35) in 1991.

• Finished among NBA top 20 in 1992 in scoring (14th, 21.0), assists (15th, 7.0) and steals (15th, 1.89).

• Career averages: 15.6 points, 6.3 rebounds, 4.9 assists.

*D*AVID ROBINSON IS NOT *your typical athlete. Nobody ever will accuse "the Admiral" of eating, sleeping, and breathing basketball. To the 7-1 center of the San Antonio Spurs, there's more to life than winning or losing a game of hoops.*

"The game's not in his blood," former Spurs assistant coach Gregg Popovich once noted. "One day I showed him something in practice. Later he said, 'I almost got it. A couple more months should do it.' He meant a concerto he was composing on his keyboard!"

Robinson's talents extend far beyond the white sidelines of the basketball floor. "Growing up, he didn't know if he wanted to be Mozart, Thomas Edison, or Bon Jovi," mused Larry Brown, who coached Robinson at San Antonio before moving on to become coach of the Los Angeles Clippers.

Robinson is the NBA's renaissance man, a graduate of the U.S. Naval Academy who loves math, science, and engineering and relaxes by playing and composing on the keyboard that is his constant companion on the NBA trail.

Robinson first achieved national attention at Annapolis, where he led the Midshipmen into the NCAA tournament and topped the nation in both rebounding and shot-blocking. The Spurs won the 1987 NBA Draft Lottery and picked Robinson, even though his military commitment meant he'd be unable to play for them for at least two years.

He showed he was worth the wait in 1990, when he led the Spurs to the Midwest Division championship and a 35-game improvement over

"**B**EING SELECTED IS EXCITING FOR ME. I'VE NOW HAD THE CHANCE TO PLAY IN THREE NBA ALL-STAR GAMES, SO I CAN IMAGINE JUST WHAT IT WILL BE LIKE (AT THE OLYMPICS) WITH EVERYBODY MORE SERIOUS AND DOING THEIR JOB."

ROBINSON

the previous season's record, the greatest single-season turnaround in NBA history. He is the premier center in the NBA today, an All-Star each of his three years in the league who excels at both ends of the floor. Robinson, like Michael Jordan and a very few others, can dominate a game offensively or defensively.

"David is the spitting image of Bill Russell," says New York Knicks Coach Pat Riley, "only David is a better athlete, and bigger. He runs the floor better. At 7 feet, he plays like he's 6-2."

Robinson tries not to think of himself as a sports superstar.

"I consider myself to be like the average guy," he said. "It's been an adjustment being a public figure. But it's just part of my profession. I try not to take on extra responsibilities. I know I can't please everyone. The only thing I think about is being the best person I can be. I try to let the kids see that. I have a God-given talent and if it doesn't work out, I'll try not to worry about it. I try to keep in close touch with who I am. That's what is important."

Robinson, who grew up in a middle-class environment in Virginia, is extemely close to his parents: Ambrose, a career Navy man, and Freda, a nurse. Together they form the Robinson Group, which handles David's local business interests since he turned professional.

"I patterned myself after my dad," said David. "I never had any sports role models. The only person I ever saw anything in was my

DAVID ROBINSON (CENTER, BACK ROW), WHO WON A BRONZE MEDAL AT THE 1988 OLYMPICS, BEGAN HIS BASKETBALL CAREER AT OSBOURN PARK HIGH SCHOOL IN MANASSAS, VIRGINIA.

dad. When I was younger, it never dawned on me what a good life I was leading. Now I see friends who don't talk to their parents, their brothers, their sisters, and I think how sad it is that they're missing out on all that love."

I'm not sure right now if Robinson knows how good he is. Can anybody else who plays center run the floor any better? Is anyone tougher defensively?

I liken him to a Bill Russell who can score. He's a great shot-blocker and a great scorer. He's big, strong, and quick, and he plays both ends of the floor well.

David gives us great flexibility. He runs so well that we can use him alongside Patrick Ewing in a two-center alignment against big opponents if we want. That kind of flexibility, as

STRENGTH AND AGILITY MAKE ROBINSON A FORCE AROUND THE BASKET FOR THE SAN ANTONIO SPURS.

I've said, is important for a coach to have.

He and Karl Malone would make an interesting race. I wouldn't be surprised if they're not quicker than any of the smaller men. Maybe we ought to schedule some 100-yard dashes and sell tickets!

Robinson is a quality individual as well, and that can only be a plus for us. We're going to be living together in a group for five weeks, and that can become difficult as time wears on. He seems to have the personality of a quiet leader whose demeanor should be helpful on a team of stars like this one, where we have so many other outgoing personalities.

Robinson is a phenomenal athlete and he certainly leads by example. He's intelligent. He wants to win. There isn't anything he can't do in the game. He's just going to get better and better and better.

ALTHOUGH HE HAD
THE OPPORTUNITY
TO TRANSFER TO
ANOTHER SCHOOL,
ROBINSON ELECTED
TO FULFILL HIS
COMMITMENT AND
GRADUATE FROM THE
U.S. NAVAL ACADEMY.

DAVID
"THE ADMIRAL"
ROBINSON

Center

San Antonio Spurs

7-1, 235, 27 years old

Birthdate: August 6, 1965

High School: Osbourn Park,

Manassas,Virginia

College: Navy

• Three-year NBA veteran.

• Three-time NBA All-Star.

• All-NBA First Team two
straight years (1991 and
1992); Third Team, 1990.

• NBA All-Defensive First
Team two straight years
(1991 and 1992); Second
Team, 1990.

• NBA Defensive Player of
the Year, 1992.

• NBA Rookie of the Year and
All-Rookie Team, 1990.

• Winner of Schick Award
for overall contributions to
team's success two straight
seasons (1990 and 1991).

• Led NBA in blocked shots
(4.49), 1992.

• Led NBA in rebounding
(13.0), 1991.

• NBA career averages:
24.4 points, 12.4 rebounds,
4.07 blocked shots.

IN SPOKANE, WASHINGTON, there's a tavern called Jack & Dan's where neighborhood residents gather on winter nights to watch Utah Jazz games via satellite. That's because Jack is the father of Jazz playmaker John Stockton, Spokane native and resident who was a local star and went on to become the top assist man in the NBA each of the last five years.

Stockton attended Gonzaga, whose most famous alumnus is Bing Crosby, because it was only a few blocks away from his home, not because he considered it a stepping stone to the NBA.

"When I was recruited by Gonzaga, they said if I ever became a pro athlete they'd be the most shocked people around," said Stockton. "I said, 'No more than me!'"

Not even his college coach, Jay Hillock, gave Stockton much of a shot at the pros. "I didn't think anyone that small could play in the NBA," Hillock said of his backcourt star, who stands barely 6-1 and weighs 175 pounds dripping wet.

But Stockton has proven that he can take it as well as dish it out in the NBA, and he always comes bouncing back for more. "He's such a relentless player," says his current coach, Jerry Sloan of the Utah Jazz. "He is much stronger than he looks."

"The guy's a competitor," said New York Knicks Coach Pat Riley. "He's always in the game. His ball-handling skills are second to none, his decision-making and running of the offense are flawless, and he has become a productive shooter. People don't think he's quick, but he'll

"I'M REALLY LOOKING FORWARD TO THE OPPORTUNITY TO PLAY FOR THE UNITED STATES IN THE OLYMPICS. I TRIED OUT FOR THE OLYMPICS WHEN I WAS IN COLLEGE AND I WAS CUT AT THE LAST CUT. IT WAS ONE OF THE BIGGEST DISAPPOINTMENTS IN MY LIFE. ALMOST MAKING THE TEAM, COMING THAT CLOSE, WAS JUST A REALLY BIG FRUSTRATION. I NEVER THOUGHT THE OPPORTUNITY TO PLAY IN THE OLYMPICS WOULD FALL BACK IN MY LAP LIKE THIS."

STOCKTON

JOHN STOCKTON'S
PASSING ABILITY HAS
MADE HIM ONE OF
THE NBA'S FINEST
POINT GUARDS AND
FLOOR LEADERS.

blow right by you. He's like a cougar, all coiled and ready to go."

Proud father Jack put it more succinctly. "He may look like an altar boy," he said, "but there's a lot of street in that kid."

Stockton learned that basketball can be a contact sport by going one-on-one against his brother Steve in the family driveway, where a brick wall was the baseline under the basket, and a white picket fence formed one sideline. "A body check into the fence or the wall developed into an acceptable form of defense," related Steve.

As a result, Stockton developed the toughness needed to go with the deft ball-handling skills which delight basketball purists. "He's a throwback to the guys who could really handle the ball, a guard like Bob Cousy," praised Utah Jazz President Frank Layden.

"He's the smartest player I've ever seen," said Jazz and Olympic teammate Karl Malone. "Nothing he does anymore surprises me. I don't know what it is he can't do, but he never tries it."

I coached in Philadelphia's Big Five for six years at Penn, and that's when the Big Five was inundated with this type of point guard—guys who may not be great physically but who see the floor well, always make the right pass, take the open shot and make it. That's the kind of guard John Stockton is, only he takes it to the ultimate level.

I think the committee saw in Stockton a guy who was totally willing to distribute the ball. Plus he can shoot threes, and he can play defense. Maybe he's not as athletically skilled as some of the other players who might have been up for this position, but I believe the committee felt that with all the talent on this team, they needed a guy who could really distribute the ball. That's what you get with him.

When he came into the league, a lot of people liked him. Yet I don't think anybody had any sense that he was going to be an All-Star. He's worked very hard to maximize the skills that he has. He gets every ounce of ability out of his body. He's a gutsy player, a hard-nosed player. He's going to get beaten sometimes

by guys with more physical ability, but he bounces right back and beats them in other ways.

I don't think he has that big an ego and that's a significant factor in his favor. Someone on this team has got to back off. We can't have everybody taking all the shots and playing all the minutes. Everybody can't try to score 20 points, not in a 40-minute game—and 20 of those minutes have to be spent on defense. You need people who are going to be willing to sacrifice their own games, and he fits the mold. Team, team, team—be part of the team and help the team win, that's what he cares about. That's so important on any team, but especially a team of stars like this.

STRONG BALL-
HANDLING SKILLS
AND A DEFT
SHOOTING TOUCH
MAKE STOCKTON
MORE THAN JUST
A PASSING FANCY.

JOHN HOUSTON STOCKTON

Guard

Utah Jazz

6-1, 175, 30 years old

Birthdate: March 26, 1962

High School: Gonzaga Prep, Spokane, Washington

College: Gonzaga

• Eight-year NBA veteran.

• Four-time NBA All-Star.

• All-NBA Second Team four times (1988, 1989, 1990, 1992); Third Team, 1991.

• NBA All-Defensive Second Team three times (1989, 1991, 1992).

• Led NBA in assists five straight seasons (1988 through 1992).

• Led NBA in steals twice (1989 and 1992).

• Set NBA record for assists in a season with 1,164 (1991).

• Only player in NBA history to compile over 1,000 assists in more than one season (five times, 1988 through 1992).

• Career averages: 12.9 points, 2.5 rebounds, 11.3 assists.

THE FIRST

EARLY LAST SEASON I was having one of my sleepless nights, which is a common occurrence among coaches. So around 1 a.m. I picked up the book *Jordan Rules* and started reading (I do this all the time), and suddenly I looked at the clock and it's 6:30 and I thought, I've got to get up and go to practice, what did I do that for? But I only had 30 or 40 more pages to go, so I figured I might as well finish it.

After reading that book (which chronicles the Chicago Bulls' 1990–91 season, when they dethroned the Detroit Pistons for the NBA title), I had a better understanding of what they went through and why they had to develop such a strong dislike for us in order to win. Underlying all their problems, everything they were going through, was us—trying to beat us. We went through it, too, when the Pistons were climbing to the top—first of all with Boston and then with the Lakers, although maybe not at the same level.

Rivalries between teams affect relationships between players in this league. There's jealousy, there's envy—you want something the other guy has, they want what you have. There's no way to avoid relationships becoming strained, given the pressures of the NBA season. That became a concern of mine as I planned for the Dream Team's first meeting at our training camp in La Jolla. I realized we were going to have to overcome rivalries if we were to succeed.

The biggest challenge of the Olympics is not necessarily

AS CAMERAMEN JOSTLE FOR POSITION, AMERICA'S DREAM TEAM LINES UP DURING CEREMONIES AT THE BASKETBALL TOURNAMENT OF THE AMERICAS.

CHALLENGE

going to be the European teams or the Asiatic team or the African team. The challenge is going to be our own people. How do we bring this team together in spirit and in thinking, as well as from a technical basketball standpoint? Will there be a clash of wills, of egos, among these stars? Will they be supportive of each other and willing to modulate their individual personalities in order to blend as a team and achieve our ultimate goal? That's going to be the challenge.

JUNE 21–26, LA JOLLA

The Dream Team came together for the first time in La Jolla, a charming California village that hugs the Pacific just north of San Diego. The Sheraton Grande Torrey Pines resort became their home, while the gymnasium on the campus of nearby UC–San Diego was their work place. Eight college basketball stars were brought in to give the USA Basketball team an opponent to scrimmage against, and four FIBA referees were imported to conduct those scrimmages and give the Dream Team a taste of international officiating. This Developmental Team, which was to play an important role in the Dream Team's training by providing a strong barometer against which to measure progress, was coached by George Raveling of Southern Cal and Roy Williams of Kansas and consisted of:

Anfernee Hardaway of Memphis State, Grant Hill and Bobby Hurley of Duke, Allan Houston of Tennessee, Jamal Mashburn of Kentucky, Eric Montross of North Carolina, Rodney Rogers of Wake Forest, and Chris Webber of Michigan.

How good were these eight? Said Daly, "I called my general manager at New Jersey, Willis Reed, and told him, 'If you spend one dime scouting any of these guys, you're wasting money. Take it from me—they all can play. They are all going to be first-round draft choices in the NBA.'" The general feeling was that in any other year, the Developmental Team, with a couple of additions, might well win the Olympic gold medal.

WHILE WAITING TO HEAD FOR PRACTICE, DAVID ROBINSON AND SCOTTIE PIPPEN (ABOVE) SELECT LINE-UP FOR A BASKETBALL VIDEO GAME. CHARLES BARKLEY (OPPOSITE) DRIVES TO THE BASKET AGAINST DAVID ROBINSON IN ONE OF THE INTRA-SQUAD SCRIMMAGES THAT SPICED PRACTICE SESSIONS IN LA JOLLA.

Developmental Team					
Player	Pos.	Ht.	Wt.	Year	College
Anfernee Hardaway	G/F	6-7	197	Jr.	Memphis State
Grant Hill	G/F	6-8	225	Jr.	Duke
Allan Houston	G	6-6	195	Sr.	Tennessee
Bobby Hurley	G	6-0	165	Sr.	Duke
Jamal Mashburn	F/C	6-8	240	Jr.	Kentucky
Eric Montross	C	7-0	258	Jr.	North Carolina
Rodney Rogers	F	6-7	235	Jr.	Wake Forest
Chris Webber	F/C	6-9	240	So.	Michigan

The Daly Routine
in La Jolla

7:15 a.m.......................Wake up, read newspapers,
review notes for day's practice.

9:15 a.m.....Go to breakfast room for tea and juice,
find out what's going on, any last-minute
things I should know.

10:15 a.m. ....Board bus for practice.

10:30 a.m. ....Practice at UC-San Diego.

12:30 p.m. ....Post-practice interviews
with the media.

1:00 p.m. ....Board bus to return to hotel.

1:15 p.m. ....Grab a light lunch.

2:00 p.m. ....Meet with coaching staff
to review practice and decide on what we're
going to emphasize in the next day's practice.

3:30 p.m...Free time.

7:30 p.m. ....Meet with coaching staff over dinner
to discuss team's progress and
other basketball matters.

10:00 p.m. ....End of day's schedule.

Then there are the telephone calls! Every time I
leave the room, when I come back there are 10 or
15 messages waiting on my voice-mail. In the
course of the day, I must get 40 or 50 calls, and
that takes time to get through. That doesn't leave
much time for golf. Then again, that's OK the way
I've been playing!

It was a relaxed, informal setting for the Dream Team—their days consisted of two hours of practice in the morning, a half-hour interview session with the media, some autograph signings with the fans who hung out in the hotel lobby or the students who gathered outside the UC–San Diego gym, then off to one of the many lush golf courses in the San Diego area. But for the coaching staff it was all (or almost all) business—their golfing was kept to a minimum.

There was less than a week of practice time before the United States would play its first game in the Basketball Tournament of the Americas. Out of this Olympic zone qualifying tournament to be held in Portland, Oregon, June 27–July 5, only 4 of 10 teams would earn berths in Barcelona. Daly and his staff knew they faced a tricky task. On the one hand, they wanted to keep things loose and easy for the players, who were coming off an arduous NBA season and needed their relaxation more than they needed to run lay-up drills. But on the other hand, there was the delicate business of molding a dozen superstars into a smoothly functioning unit, one that would have to compete under international rules with which they were unaccustomed and against opponents whose ultimate dream was to beat the supposedly unbeatable USA Dream Team.

Thus, as the players began to check in on Sunday, June 21, it was no surprise to find Daly up in his room. While suite 4117 had a marvelous view of the Torrey Pines golf course and the blue Pacific beyond, Daly's focus was on his outline for the initial meeting with the players that night. It was the team's first face-to-face gathering, and Daly saw it as a vital opportunity to set the tone for the weeks ahead.

I had thought a lot about this. I knew I had to do some selling. There had to be a clear understanding of why we'd come together; I just hoped we could convey the seriousness of the situation. It wasn't life and death, of course, just basketball. But we were serious about this particular endeavor. There's an old saying in our league: coaches get paid to win, players get paid to play. This was different. Here the burden for winning was on

Working Out
with the Dream Team

Here's what a typical practice schedule looked like (this one is from Thursday, June 25, when the team was training in La Jolla):

10:15 a.m. ....Leave hotel

10:30 a.m. ....Meeting & stretch

10:45 a.m. ....Half-court lay-up drill

10:50 a.m. ....5-on-0 review

10:55 a.m. .....4-on-4 touch the line fast break drill

11:05 a.m. ....5-on-5 defense

("Blast"offense/Transition)

11:15 a.m. ....Twenty minute half

(Developmental Team)

11:50 a.m. ....Ten minute scrimmage

(Developmental Team)

12:15 p.m. ....Introduce "15" offensive set

12:30 p.m. ...Practice ends, media interviews begin

1:00 p.m. ....Return to hotel

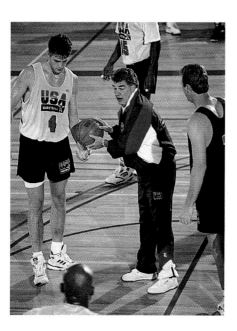

every single person in the group, players and coaches. It was paramount that we understand there was only one goal and we all would have to make some sort of sacrifice.

I had a little spadework to do before the actual meeting—I wanted to talk to two or three people in an effort to create some internal leadership. Magic Johnson and Larry Bird were the obvious candidates to be our co-captains, because of their personalities, their achievements, their "elder statesmen" role in the league. But I also wanted to see if Michael Jordan, given all the demands on him, would be interested. So before our first team meeting I went to Michael and asked, "Do you want to be involved in a leadership triumvirate?" And he said no, he agreed with our idea that those two guys are the elder statesmen; they've been leaders in the league for many years, and they're the two guys who should assume the leadership role on the team—although obviously, Michael still would be very prominent in terms of leading by example.

I thought we had a terrific first meeting. It lasted some two hours and touched on many areas of concern, most of them off the basketball court. As a staff, we had tried to cover as many of these things as possible—meals, places we'll be staying, transportation, things like that. I had several handouts that I prepared for the players, because I wanted to make sure they understood the schedule for the summer. I wasn't going to assume anything. After all, they had just been through a rigorous season, paying attention to their own business, and now the Olympic effort was upon them.

We talked about the amount of media that would be following this team, as many as 6,000 or more at Barcelona. We talked about general security procedures, which become very important at a high-profile event like this. And then we talked about other things more directly related to basketball, like practice schedules, international rules, injuries, and actual aspects of the game. When we broke up, I felt really good about the meeting and about the way the players were approaching this endeavor.

Originally, I had thought a couple of guys who had been named to the team in September wouldn't be available because of injuries. To me that seemed inevitable, given the rigors of the NBA season. But what I found out was, once they got the invitation, there was no way they were giving it up. If they could drag themselves in here on hands and knees, they were going to those Games! So one thing we had to do in practice was evaluate the physical condition of some of the players—who was ready to go and who wasn't.

We were thinking seriously about using a different starting team each night, in order to keep more people involved. There had to be an understanding that 40 minutes is a very limited amount of time to play all of these people. But then, it's not that different from any night in an NBA season, where every player wants 48 minutes and 48 shots.

Monday was our first practice, always a big day for a coaching staff. The temptation is to practice your players too hard, but you have to learn to pull back. My outline had us leaving for practice at 10 and breaking at 12:30 or 12:45. I realized that that was a little longer than I wanted to go. I looked at it and decided that this wasn't going to be as much fun for the players as I thought it would be. We might have to make some adjustments!

I was really impressed with the enthusiasm I saw during our first practice. There was almost too much energy. They were very hyper, trying to do too much. They were over-passing, as if they were making a conscious effort to defer to one another and not look like one guy was trying to grab the spotlight. For the most part, they were better conditioned than I thought they'd be, and some of them surprised me by being in better shape than I had expected.

No question, this was the greatest group of individual

CHRIS MULLIN RESTS ON AN EXERCISE BIKE WHILE AWAITING THE START OF PRACTICE AT THE UC-SAN DIEGO GYM.

basketball talents ever assembled. As coaches our job was to bring them together as a team, so we put in some skeletal things to start to give them a framework in which to operate. I thought that was essential—we didn't want players running around out there relying only on their pure ability. We had to give them a framework. But these players were so talented, we as coaches had to be careful to keep a light hold on the reins and not try to over-organize.

The next day we were still over-passing and not protecting the ball. You can't afford that because every time you turn the ball over in international play you give the other team a chance at a three-pointer, and that can kill you. Defensively we weren't playing the three-point line well yet. We had to coach them to stay home with their opponents and not double the post when the ball goes inside, which is instinctive in our league.

People keep asking about the rules differences and what effect that can have, and I always say that's something you just have to adjust to as best you can. You can't change the way you play a game you've played your entire life in a matter of days, or even weeks.

The shorter three-point line is the most obvious difference. We would have to be conscious of stopping other teams from taking threes, as well as spotting up at the line when we had the ball. Sure it's a very makeable shot for most of our players, but they're not accustomed to looking for it because the distance in the NBA is longer. We shoot it, but not constantly. Teams in Europe set up for it constantly. This was something we would have to learn to deal with offensively and defensively, and it wouldn't become automatic in such a short period of time.

The 40-minute game clock is a tremendous difference for us. I watch a European game, and bang, it's over before I know it! Frankly, that's a little frightening because anything can happen in a game of 40 minutes. You get a team that's shooting well, you'd

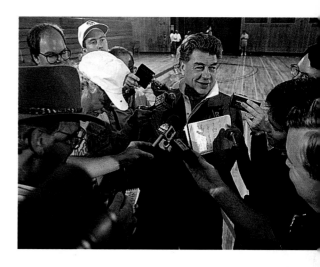

DALY UPDATES THE MEDIA ON THE DAY'S WORKOUT. IN ORDER TO LESSEN DISTRAC- TIONS, ALL BUT THE LAST 15 MINUTES OF EACH PRACTICE WAS CLOSED.

better be ready to defend them at the three-point line, because the game could be over before you realize what has happened.

I like the trapezoidal lane, even though it's only a difference of 2 1/2 to 3 inches on a line of 45 inches from a post-up standpoint. It creates more freedom for cutting under the basket. I think it's something the NBA should look into to eliminate some of the low-post sumo wrestling that goes on in our league.

I didn't think the 30-second shot clock (instead of the NBA's 24-second clock) would be much of a factor, and I also didn't think zone defenses would bother us. These players are so talented, so quick, and such great shooters, I didn't think they could be stopped by a zone. Timeouts would be significant because you only get two per half, and substitution patterns could be a problem because it's much harder to get players into the game. As for being allowed to touch the ball after it hits the rim even if it's above the basket, or not being allowed to catch an

ASSISTANT COACH P.J. CARLESIMO GOES TO THE DRAWING BOARD TO DIAGRAM WHERE EACH PLAYER IS SUPPOSED TO GO IN VARIOUS PLAYS.

alley-oop pass above the rim, those are subtleties that I was not sure we would to be able to incorporate in the short time we had to adjust. And since we were unfamiliar with the international game, the officiating could be a problem, so I told our players they had to learn to get past mad, not get caught up in anything and just play their game.

We held scrimmages against the Developmental Team at the end of practice on Monday and Tuesday, and on Tuesday it was clear—even though we did not keep score—that the college kids were taking things seriously and playing really well. So we decided at a staff meeting Tuesday night to put time and score up on the board the next day, so we could all see where we were. We also asked Roy Williams and George Raveling to have their team shoot the three as much as possible, because I knew we needed to become more conscious of the three-point line.

So what happened? We gave up 30 points on three-pointers and were outscored 62-54 in Wednesday's 20-minute scrimmage. Yes, the Dream Team of NBA All-Stars was outplayed and outscored by a group of eight college underclassmen—and since we had put it up on the board, there was no way to ignore it! Afterwards I found out that our players were more than a little upset by the way they had played, and I was pleased by that reaction—they had every right to be upset, just like I was!

ASSISTANT COACH LENNY WILKENS STUDIES A SCRIM-MAGE WITH THE PRACTICED EYE THAT COMES FROM MORE THAN THREE DECADES AS AN NBA PLAYER AND COACH.

That scrimmage served as a nice little wake-up call for our team, and the next day we had an absolutely great practice. The difference in the team was like night and day. Offensively and defensively we were in much better sync, and our confidence level was back up where it should be. The Developmental Team had been hurting us with three-pointers, and we had told our guys what they had to do. But sometimes saying it and seeing it are two different things. On Wednesday they saw it up on the scoreboard, and by Thursday they had decided to do something about it.

We were still throwing the ball away too much, but that was largely because these guys are so talented, they think they can make any pass. I kept telling them, "Make the simple pass," but it's too easy for them to make an A to B pass. They insist on trying to make A to B through C, because even though it's more difficult, they're confident enough to think they can do it.

You have to remember, all the players on this team are go-to guys on their respective teams. Now they go out there and look around at their teammates for the Olympic Games and find they don't have to do quite as much. Understanding this and backing off was not easy early on, but by Thursday I saw rapid advancement.

I have to say, I was more than a little concerned after Wednesday's practice, but one day later I felt a lot better about where we were. I think everyone did—Thursday's scrimmage was a big turning point for us.

One tough thing did happen in practice: Patrick Ewing had his finger cut and displaced when it got slammed against the rim, and that scared everybody. But the medical reports were encouraging, and he was expected to be OK after a few days.

Friday was getaway day, with the team holding a morning practice and then flying up to Portland, where we were to be honored in a gala "Golden Moments" dinner before some 1,500

THE VIEW FROM THE SIDELINES AS DALY PUTS MEMBERS OF THE DREAM TEAM THROUGH A FULL-COURT, 3-ON-3 DRILL.

people at the Oregon Convention Center. We had another good
practice and a good scrimmage against the Developmental
Team, and I left La Jolla feeling very positive. We had
accomplished a lot in five days, but I found that from a coaching
standpoint there are just too many situations that you can't cover.
I caught myself going overtime in practice, day in and day out,

until Friday when we were forced to stop because we had a
plane to catch.

*There was no sign of a clash of egos in La Jolla, much to the relief of
the coaching staff. These players, most of whom had never spent any
extended time together, got along well, spending much of their free time
in foursomes of golf, going into town for dinner, or playing cards.*

*Johnson quickly assumed the mantle of leadership. During one of
the team's early practices, when things weren't going well, he stopped
everybody in the middle of play and called the team together for a pep
talk. Jordan blended in nicely with his new "supporting cast" and
praised Daly's loose hand on the reins—a hand that enabled MJ to get
in 36 holes of golf on some days. A friendship blossomed between
Ewing and Bird, who dubbed themselves "Harry and Larry" in their
own version of the much-ballyhooed decathletes Dan and Dave.*

*Even Laettner, the outsider from the college ranks, was accepted into
the fold. At the gym he showed he could hold his own with the pros,
impressing them with his willingness to hit the boards and versatility in
playing all three front-court positions. Off the court he was accepted as
well. One night when the card game was about to start, the players
realized they were missing a key ingredient, namely a deck of cards, so
Barkley promptly dispatched Laettner to round one up. That was the*

EVEN AFTER ONLY
A FEW PRACTICES, IT
BECOMES APPARENT
TO DALY AND HIS
STAFF THAT TEAM
MEMBERS WOULD
HAVE NO TROUBLE
GETTING ALONG.

closest he came to any rookie hazing in La Jolla.

By the time the players took off to Portland on Friday afternoon, they had made great strides in coming together as a team.

JUNE 27-JULY 5, PORTLAND

Upon arriving in Portland, my feeling was that it was time to get on with the competition. We needed to play a real game so that we as coaches and the players could see exactly where we were from a conditioning standpoint and from an organization standpoint, and to find out once and for all what it was going to be like to compete at an international level.

We all enjoyed Saturday's opening ceremonies and the warm reception we got from the crowd and even from the opposing players, many of whom were eager to shake hands and take pictures with our guys.

Finally, on Sunday, we got to play our first game, and it was a very good first outing for us. We beat Cuba, a team that didn't have much size but did have some quickness, 136–57. I had a pretty good idea, having coached in an All-Star Game, how our players would come out. In every one of our practices they had been very intense, and that's how they came out against Cuba. I told them we had to play defense, hit the open man, rebound and run, and we did all of those things and did them well.

WHEREVER AMERICA'S DREAM TEAM WENT, IT WAS THE CENTER OF ATTENTION. DALY PEERS OUT A WINDOW OF THE TEAM BUS AT PART OF THE CROWD THAT KEPT A CONSTANT VIGIL OUTSIDE THE VINTAGE HOTEL IN PORTLAND, THE TEAM'S HEAD-QUARTERS. EVEN OPPOSING PLAYERS SHOW DELIGHT IN MEETING U.S. STARS LIKE MAGIC JOHNSON AND CLYDE DREXLER.

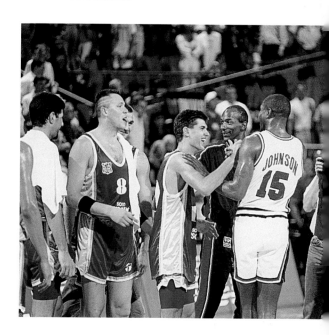

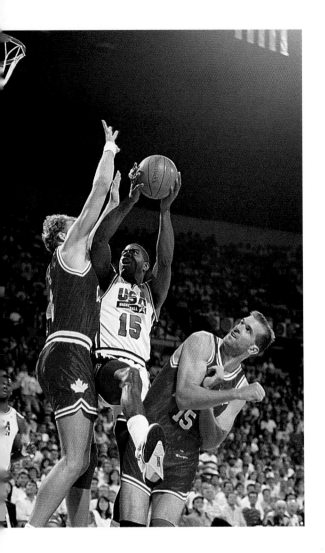

IN HIS FIRST
EXTENDED COMPETI-
TION (OTHER THAN
THE ALL-STAR GAME)
IN MORE THAN A
YEAR, JOHNSON
SHOWS THAT HE
HAS NOT LOST HIS
MAGIC TOUCH.

PREVIOUS SPREAD:
CHARLES BARKLEY
(NO. 14) IS ABOUT TO
SNARE A REBOUND
DURING THE U.S.
TEAM'S 136–57 ROUT
OF CUBA IN THE
TOURNAMENT
OPENER, AS MAGIC
JOHNSON AND LARRY
BIRD LOOK ON.

After the game I was asked about whether I had tried to slow our players down in order to keep the score from being so lopsided. I said I hadn't, because we've got to play the game as best we can, otherwise why bother? I don't know how you can tell players not to play; I don't think other teams would want us to play them at half-speed.

On Monday we played Canada, a team with several big guys who had played in the NBA—Bill Wennington, Mike Smrek, and Leo Rautins. I don't think we came out quite as energeti-cally as we did against Cuba, and we let them hang around a little bit, but we picked it up in the second half, particularly defensively, and won easily 105–61.

I had told them before the Canada game that I thought the opening game was a Picasso. The second one wasn't quite as good. We dropped some balls, and we missed some shots at the end of the break. We weren't quite as sharp as we were Sunday, and I kind of expected that.

Would the lopsided scores of our first two games make motivation a problem? It was entirely possible, although we discussed at halftime about not playing to anyone else's level. It would be important that we continue to play at our level, regardless of the score.

Injuries were becoming a concern. Larry Bird did not play Monday because his back stiffened up, which is a problem that would force his retirement after the Olympics. John Stockton got hit on the upper part of the right calf, and while at first it didn't look any worse than a charley horse, X-rays showed a non-displaced fracture of the right fibula. Dr. David Fischer, our team physician, said he would be out for the rest of the Portland tournament. The good news was that Patrick Ewing came to us and said his injured hand felt better. He was cleared by the doctors to play, so we were able to get him some minutes on Monday.

On Tuesday we played Panama, which was clearly outsized. They tried to keep the score close by taking good care of the ball and packing in a zone, and that worked until they started missing some shots. We changed personnel, and Chris Mullin did a terrific job hitting some threes, as did Michael Jordan. We had a lot of really good shots against the zone defense and were able to control the game and win 112–52.

As I said earlier, the zone didn't worry me. Every time we played against it we would get a little more comfortable, and I knew we had the personnel to beat it. Frankly, we had so many people who could dribble right up, bang, and make that three-point shot, that a zone couldn't be effective. One of the areas where the selection committee did an outstanding job was making sure we had enough outside shooters. We had to have people who could make the three, and we got them.

I was happy with the team's attitude. For the most part, they had stayed away from "Showtime." They seemed to read the other team and do what was needed against them.

We played our fourth game in four nights on Wednesday and beat Argentina 128–87 with only nine players. Besides Larry and John, Clyde Drexler sat out with a bruised knee, an injury he had late in the season, too. As it turned out there were no serious foul problems, so we were able to win by rotating our nine people.

INJURIES BECAME A CONCERN FOR THE DREAM TEAM. JOHN STOCKTON SHOWS THE MEDIA WHERE HE SUFFERED THE BROKEN BONE IN HIS LEG, WHILE LARRY BIRD TAKES EVERY OPPORTUNITY TO REST HIS CHRONI-CALLY SORE BACK.

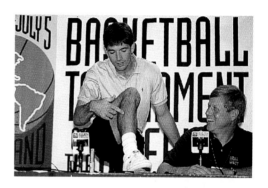

Rules Differences

RULE	FIBA	NBA	NCAA
Game duration	2 20-minute halves	4 12-minute quarters	2 20-minute halves
Shot clock	30 seconds	24 seconds	45 seconds
Court length	91'10" x 49'2.5"	94'0" x 50'	94'0" x 50'
Lane size	19'8.2" x 19'0.3" (trapezoid)	16' x 19' (rectangle)	12' x 19' (rectangle)
3-pt. FG distance	20'6.1"	23'9"	19'9"
Player foul limit	5	6	5
Bonus free throw	8th team foul per half	5th team foul per quarter	7th team foul per half
Time outs	2 each half	7 per game	5 per game
Jump ball	Yes	Yes	No; teams alternate positions
Legal alley-oop	No	Yes	Yes
Touch ball on cylinder	Yes	No	No

It was a typical game. The Argentines wanted to slow it down and played zone defense, but I just don't think you can do that against us. I'm not sure what anyone could have done. I loved the Cuban coach's statement, "You cannot cover the sun with your finger." We just had so many weapons; truthfully, it was very, very difficult for these teams to cover all our weapons.

We experimented for the first time with using our two centers together. It was something we had talked about as a coaching staff some weeks ago in Colorado Springs. We thought that using Patrick Ewing and David Robinson together could give us a very interesting lineup with two major league shot blockers. It's a pressure team, a shot-blocking team, and I thought it was pretty effective.

After a day off on Thursday in which just about everyone hit the golf course—people were calling Pumpkin Ridge the unofficial headquarters of the Dream Team—we beat Puerto Rico 119–81 in the semifinals on Friday. I didn't think we played with a lot of emotion, but we didn't have to after we got out to a good lead. The talent of our players just seemed to take over the game after about 10 minutes.

For some reason, other teams didn't seem to play us the same way they played each other. Maybe they were too much in awe of us, but they didn't compete like I'd seen them against other teams. And that made it difficult to gauge where we were because we had been able to pretty much control each game. We had not yet been tested.

Saturday, the Fourth of July, was another day off, then we beat Venezuela 127–80 in the finals on Sunday. Venezuela was coming off two emotional highs. They beat Canada on Thursday to qualify for the Olympics for the first time in the country's history. Then they beat Brazil on Friday to reach the finals. But they were in awe of us. Their coach, Julio Toro, said before the finals that we were "the geniuses of the game" and that for

SCOTTIE PIPPEN (BELOW) AND CHRIS MULLIN (OPPOSITE) PROVIDE THE VERSA- TILITY AND DEPTH TO OVERCOME INJURIES, SINCE EACH CAN PLAY GUARD OR FORWARD.

Venezuela, "the silver is the gold because the U.S. team is from another planet." So we took his cue and scored the first 15 points of the game, and it was never close.

Although none of the games were competitive after the first 10 minutes and the U.S. defeated its six opponents by an average of 51.5 points per game, the Basketball Tournament of the Americas was a big success. It drew tremendous TV ratings for its four telecasts on NBC and TNT, and the fans in Portland were thrilled to have had the chance to see the Dream Team in action. The same was true for the team's rivals, who came up with a new pre-game ritual by posing for a two-team photograph minutes before the tipoff of each game against the USA squad.

Marcelo Milanesio, Argentina's point guard, summed up the rival players' feelings when he said, "Without any doubt, not just for us but for everyone playing in this tournament, it is great to play with Michael Jordan and Magic Johnson. I am so overwhelmed with joy."

"They are all my idols," said Oscar Schmidt of Brazil, the leading scorer in the Italian pro league in 1991–92. "Michael Jordan to me is the best player in the world. But Larry Bird is my biggest idol. He is what all players who play shooting forward would like to be. I want his autograph!"

After hearing that, Boston Globe *columnist Bob Ryan dug up a copy of* Drive, *the Bird autobiography he co-authored, and Bird inscribed it: "I want you 1-on-1 in French Lick!" Schmidt's reaction, after oohing and ahhing, was: "What is this French Lick?" Apparently word of Bird's hometown in Indiana, and his backyard basketball court, had not reached Brazil.*

USA forward Karl Malone found some of the adulation a bit odd. The Mailman watched in disbelief as Magic Johnson posted up a smaller Argentinian player who, instead of concentrating on his defense, was posing for a photograph. "He was looking at a teammate on the bench who was taking the picture. That's a bit much, don't you think?" said Malone.

Overall, we had a very interesting two weeks, both during the training camp in La Jolla and the tournament in Portland. We controlled the tournament games from the outset and did a good job of doing the things we wanted to do each day. Now the focus became Barcelona, where we sensed there would be more competition. We were looking forward to the challenge. As Magic said after we beat Venezuela, this was only the beginning, the real job was still ahead of us. We had some people scouting the European qualifying tournament, and over the next two

CHRISTIAN LAETTNER (OPPOSITE) SHOWS HE CAN PLAY WITH THE PROS, BLOCKING A SHOT BY PUERTO RICO'S JOSE ORTIZ. AND WHILE THE COACHES NEVER LOST THEIR GAME FACES, IT QUICKLY BECOMES APPARENT IN THE FINALS AT PORTLAND THAT NOBODY ON THE VENEZUELAN TEAM HAS THE SIZE OR STRENGTH TO STOP PATRICK EWING.

weeks we would look at films of their games and get some rest before we resumed training in Monaco on July 20.

Regarding the injuries, John and Larry headed home to undergo rehabilitation. We had no real doubt that both of them would be with us in Barcelona.

I think that what was most interesting for me those two weeks was the bonding that took place among the players on the team. They really came together and enjoyed themselves on and off the court, more so than you might imagine for such high-profile stars. If I learned one thing it was that they are really good people, fun to be around.

I don't think you can even sense how great these players really are. I've been in the league some 15 years now and I still marvel, even in these games which were not very competitive, at some of the things these people are capable of doing. We really are seeing the greatest players in the history of the game, and it's a joy to be part of it.

AFTER THE MEDALS WERE DISTRIBUTED, THE FLAG RAISED, AND THE ANTHEM PLAYED IN THE CLOSING CERE-MONIES AT PORT-LAND, BIRD AND JOHNSON PROUDLY POSE WITH THEIR GOLD MEDALS.

THE MAGIC OF EARVIN JOHNSON

*E*ARVIN JOHNSON'S SMILE *has lit the sports world for more than a decade. The pure joy he has shown in playing the game he loves is something we all have shared, and been enriched by. Johnson burst upon the national consciousness as a precocious 19-year-old in 1979 when, as a sophomore, he led Michigan State to the national collegiate title. He has brought pleasure to billions worldwide; it is a feeling no disease ever can erase.*

Last October in Paris, where the Lakers competed against three of Europe's finest club teams in the 1991 McDonald's Open, Johnson was besieged by fans wherever he went. From the Champs Elysees to the Tour d'Eiffel to the Bateaux Mouches along the Seine, for 10 days he savored being an American in Paris, accompanied by his recent bride, Cookie, pregnant at the time with their first child. Chants of "Magique! Magique!" filled the Palais Omnisports de Bercy as the Lakers won the tournament and Johnson earned MVP honors. He closed the event's final media session on October 19 by telling the assembled writers, "Thanks for everything, I've had a great time. I'll see you in Barcelona!"

Less than three weeks later, on November 7, Johnson shocked the world—not just the sports world—by announcing that he had tested

*positively for the HIV virus that causes AIDS. A life that had truly
been magical, a life of athletic success and public adulation few ever
experience, had been touched by tragedy. There he stood in the Forum
Club in the Lakers' home building, the Great Western Forum, the same
room where for so many years he had mingled with and accepted plau-
dits from Tinseltown's glitterati following Laker victories, saying it
was all over. "Because of the HIV virus I have attained, I will have to
announce my retirement from the Lakers today," he solemnly told an
audience that only wanted to hear him say it wasn't so.*

*It was a stunning moment, one of the most unsettling pronounce-
ments in sports history. Never before had such a renowned figure ever
come forward and made such a statement, and the news conference
was televised live by both CNN and ESPN. The reaction was swift,
the news bringing front-page, banner headlines worldwide. The
Spanish daily* El Pais *ran two pages on "The Magic Man: A Living
Legend and a Myth in World Sport," while another Spanish paper,*
ABC, *wrote that the news was "like a jug of cold water on all corners
of the globe, where the Lakers' guard was seen as a shining example of
an upright, honest, and human sportsman." Portuguese television*

WITH HIS WIFE,
COOKIE, BY HIS SIDE,
MAGIC JOHNSON
STUNNED THE
WORLD WHEN HE
ANNOUNCED THAT
HE HAD CONTRACTED
THE HIV VIRUS THAT
CAUSES AIDS AND
THAT HE WOULD BE
RETIRING FROM THE
LOS ANGELES LAKERS.

said, "His words have made tears fall around the world," and a Tokyo daily headline proclaimed, "It's A Tragedy."

Over time, the reaction to Johnson's announcement would come in three waves. Here's the way Magic's agent and long-time friend, Lon Rosen, describes it:

"In the beginning there was a tremendous outpouring of support. We were inundated with phone calls, letters, faxes, from regular fans all the way to the President. Everyone initially was very supportive.

"After those initial good feelings, we started to hear some negative things. People began to take shots at him, saying it's wrong to make him into a hero just because he got the AIDS virus. Then it went back again the other way. Most people recognized that he had done something very courageous by coming forward and being so open about his disease, instead of hiding it like so many other people had done. A few people

JOHNSON'S NEWS BROUGHT THOU- SANDS OF LETTERS OF SUPPORT (ABOVE). THE LAKERS RETIRED HIS UNIFORM NO. 32 IN A CEREMONY AS HIS FAMILY LOOKED ON (BELOW).

are still going to take shots at him, that's never going to stop. But
99 percent of the world has been supportive in light of the way he's
handled the situation."

Earvin Johnson's nickname, coined by a local sports writer when he was still at Everett High School in Lansing, Michigan, says it all. On and off the court, there is a certain quality about him that can best be described as Magic.

One of the most talented and charismatic athletes ever to play our game, Magic Johnson's impact on the NBA cannot be overstated. When he and Larry Bird became pros in 1979, the league was in a flat period. They just picked it right up and took it to a higher level. They set the table for Michael Jordan, Karl Malone, and the other great players of the '90s. The way Magic and Larry play the game, their emphasis on passing and team play, made

JOHNSON HAS TRIED TO CONVINCE PRESIDENT BUSH TO INCREASE SPENDING ON RESEARCH INTO THE PREVENTION AND CURE OF AIDS.

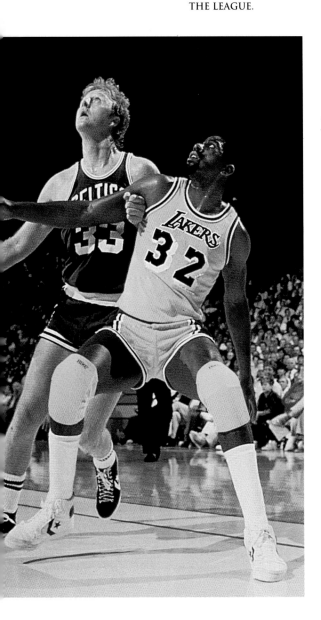

UPON ENTERING THE NBA TOGETHER IN 1979, JOHNSON AND LARRY BIRD USHERED IN AN ERA OF UNPRECEDENTED POPULARITY AND PROSPERITY FOR THE LEAGUE.

millions of new fans for professional basketball.

From the time he first gained national attention at Michigan State, Magic had something special about him. Anybody could see it. His smile, his sparkle, his obvious delight in playing the game of basketball was readily apparent to me as well as to everyone else connected with the sport. It's always a joy to see someone doing what he loves, and doing it better than anyone else. For me that sums up Magic Johnson.

The 1979 NCAA final between Magic's Michigan State Spartans and Larry's Indiana State Sycamores was a landmark event in basketball history. Their showdown really captured the public's imagination, to the extent that more than a decade later it still ranks among the most-watched basketball games of all time. The build-up for that meeting was so monumental, few people seemed to mind that the game itself was somewhat anti-climactic, with Michigan State just being too strong overall for the upstart Sycamores.

Magic liked to use a phrase that was later picked up by sports writers Scott Ostler and Steve Springer as the title of a book about the Lakers of the 1980s: *Winnin' Time*. Winning has always been what Magic was all about. He was the key player in the Lakers' surge to five NBA championships during the 1980s, the fulcrum around which the "Team of the '80s" revolved. How many times have we all seen Magic streaking down the Forum floor in the middle of the Lakers' fast break, looking one way and then dishing the other to James Worthy or Michael Cooper or Byron Scott for a stuff? It was "Showtime" at its best, and it never failed to bring the crowd to its feet because it was beauti-ful to watch—except when I was coaching the team on the visitors' bench and had to try to find a way to stop it! I couldn't, not for any great length of time, and nobody else could either.

Then came his announcement that he had tested HIV posi-tive, and like everyone else I was shocked. The closest thing I

can compare it to is the day I was sitting in the Duke basketball office—I was a freshman coach with Bucky Waters, who is now a TV commentator—and we got the announcement of the death of President Kennedy. I know there's a difference between an athlete getting the HIV virus and the death of a President, but my point is this: there are rare moments in your life when you are so taken aback and so shocked by an event, and these were two moments like that. There had been rumors about it for at least a week before, because Magic had sat out some pre-season games, but you dismiss them and say it just can't possibly be true. But that morning I heard about the press conference, so I made sure I was available to see what was going on.

Magic is an individual who has tremendous ability, charisma, and will to win—truly a once-in-a-lifetime player, because to find those three qualities embodied in one individual is very rare. And he's always been a gentleman, one of the most courteous and caring athletes we have. So I sat there stunned, listening to his announcement. Then you start to think in terms like, did this come from a higher source to alert us to this particular disease? Clearly AIDS is a serious problem in our society and in the world, and maybe this was our wake-up call.

As far as the Olympic team was concerned, initially I didn't know what to think. Like most people, basically I was pretty ignorant about the disease. We had to learn all about it. I wasn't sure if he was going to be able to play, but I thought it would be great to have him around in some capacity, even if he couldn't play. He still could be very valuable in terms of helping us as coaches deal with the players if we ran into problems.

So there was never any question in my mind that he was

A LAKERS HALL OF FAME (FROM LEFT). OWNER JERRY BUSS, GM JERRY WEST, WILT CHAMBERLAIN, MAGIC JOHNSON, KAREEM ABDUL-JABBAR, AND ELGIN BAYLOR.

going to be part of the overall experience. I wanted him around because he has incredible leadership qualities, and I knew they would enhance whatever we were trying to do.

There was never any question in Johnson's mind, either, that he would be around—and as a player.

"No question whatsoever," he said, shaking his head, when asked about it at the team's La Jolla, California, training camp. "I never doubted that I would be ready to compete in the Olympics, not for one moment. That goal is what kept me going through those many workouts. Playing in the Olympics was my motivation.

"This is even bigger than an NBA championship because in the Olympics you're playing for the whole United States, not just a small portion of it. For me, this would mean I would have accomplished everything in basketball—winning the NCAA title, the NBA title, and the Olympics.

"Finally getting a chance to play with all these guys means a great deal to me, especially Larry [Bird] after what we've been through. It would be fitting for us to go out together, if this is to be the last chapter. Our careers are locked together, with the NCAA finals, those three NBA finals between the Lakers and Celtics, our rivalry through the '80s. I never thought, in my wildest dreams, that Larry and I would ever be able to play together for something like this.

"I'm just enjoying every minute of it. This could be the last hurrah for both of us. So this one isn't just for Lakers fans or just for Celtics fans, this time it's going to be for all basketball fans everywhere."

Rosen, Magic's agent, watched him work each day to stay sharp. "He used the Olympics to motivate himself. He kept himself in incredible shape, working out constantly. And these weren't light workouts—he rented Pauley Pavilion at UCLA or Loyola Marymount and played hard, full-court basketball for three months with people like Gary Grant, Reggie Miller, Pooh Richardson, Shaquille O'Neal, Larry Drew—good players. He wanted to be sure that when he came to camp in La Jolla in June, he would be prepared

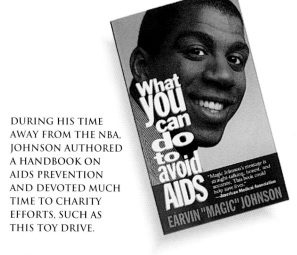

DURING HIS TIME AWAY FROM THE NBA, JOHNSON AUTHORED A HANDBOOK ON AIDS PREVENTION AND DEVOTED MUCH TIME TO CHARITY EFFORTS, SUCH AS THIS TOY DRIVE.

to participate at the same level as when he left the NBA.

"There was never any question in his mind about the Olympics. The doubts were in other people's minds, and he used that as further motivation. When people like IOC President Juan Antonio Samaranch, or that Australian doctor, or Bob Ferry and Peter Vecsey on NBC said there were questions whether he'd be able to participate, Earvin didn't get mad. He just became more determined to prove them wrong."

Meanwhile, Johnson was busier than ever off the court. He authored a well-received AIDS-prevention handbook that was published last spring and an autobiography, "My Life," with William Novak, which is due this winter. He also taped an AIDS-awareness special on Nickelodeon with Linda Ellerbe, aimed at educating youngsters about the disease, and a video with Arsenio Hall. He filled requests from charities too numerous to mention.

"Earvin takes the charity requests in stride, because that's something that has always been there," said Rosen. "He has always done a lot for charity; last year he did more because he had more time because he wasn't playing in the league. What he's really putting a lot of time and effort into is education, particularly with inner-city youth, because he feels he can have the greatest impact within the black community."

AFTER NOT PLAYING DURING THE REGULAR SEASON, JOHNSON MADE A FANTASY COMEBACK BY WINNING MVP HONORS AT THE 1992 ALL-STAR GAME.

As I watched him at the All-Star Game, Magic dismissed all doubts about his playing when he had 25 points and was the MVP. He was terrific, both in the way he played on the court and in the way he handled himself off the court, where he constantly was surrounded by fans and media. As for the game, that was not a set-up situation—these guys have too much pride for that. Magic flat-out earned the MVP.

Then I was really pleased to see his condition when he came to the Olympic training camp in La Jolla. Right away I could see he was in great shape, having worked out on a daily basis, built his upper body, and played a lot of pick-up basketball. After our first scrimmage I could tell that Magic hadn't missed a beat. He was basically the same player he always was, only now he was trying harder because he felt he had more to prove. He was as well-conditioned as anybody in camp. I saw no flaws in his ability to play whatsoever. Magic's enthusiasm was terrific. He has such great drive and desire, I was not concerned about him at all.

Quite simply, it is an honor to be coaching Magic with this team. He's given so much to the game, been one of our great players and one of our leading ambassadors for so long. He's very special.

More than a year ago, when the Olympic team first was announced, I spoke with Magic by phone and he said something which I thought was very important. He said, "We're going to go through the season and we're going to have tough competition among some of the players on this team. So we need to establish some sort of a social atmosphere." He suggested that when we got together for training camp in La Jolla, we do some other

NEVER ONE TO CONTAIN HIS ENTHU-SIASM, JOHNSON LEAPS OFF THE BENCH TO CONGRAT-ULATE MICHAEL JORDAN DURING THE BASKETBALL TOURNAMENT OF THE AMERICAS.

things besides practice—maybe play golf together, have a cook-out, or whatever. Just do some things together to heal whatever wounds had been opened up during the previous year or over the years, to try to bring this team together. Magic's thinking was that if we created a good social atmosphere, it would be easier to handle any of the other problems, like distributing minutes, points, etc.

I thought that was great. This was like frosting on the cake for the coaches—right then we knew that our jobs, as coaches, would be easier with Magic around.

Mike LoPresti, a columnist for the Gannett papers, watched Johnson compete at the Basketball Tournament of the Americas in Portland and led a story this way: "He looks the same. He acts the same. He plays the same. The man at the point for the U.S. Olympic basketball team is Magic Johnson, and nothing about him is different. Basketball-wise, anyway. And if that is a surprise, it is our fault, not his."

Which is what Johnson had been saying all along.

"The greatest feeling is that I can be Magic again," he reflected while in Portland. "The whole year I had to answer questions and I couldn't show people. I had to just sit there and answer questions over and over and over again. Now they can see it. It's happening and I'm loving every minute of it. This is where I belong, on the basketball floor.

"Everything I could do, I can still do. I noticed it [during work-outs], but you guys had to see it. So here it is. All I want to show is I'm back playing basketball again."

Johnson played brilliantly in Portland, leading the tournament with 54 assists and playing 144 minutes, more than any other U.S. player. He was, indeed, Magic again—on the fast break, directing traffic and throwing no-look passes with his customary flair, erasing any doubts that might have lingered in the minds of skeptics.

"The light has been off for me for a long while, and I'm switching it back on," he declared. "I'm a challenge man. I love challenges. That's what I've been about my whole career. Like the All-Star Game, people

JOHNSON SHOWED DURING THE SUMMER OF '92 THAT HE HAD LOST NONE OF HIS BALLHANDLING MAGIC.

saying, 'No, he shouldn't play, what's going to happen?' That was a challenge, then bam, it's over, count the stats!

"Now this challenge. More questions were being raised, so I'm meeting that right now. I always knew what I could do. When you're working out, it's harder than the game—this is the easy part."

Johnson carried the flag for the U.S. team at the Basketball Tournament of the Americas and said he "had goose bumps all over. You always dream of what's going to happen when you get a chance like this, but this was better by far, much greater than my expectations. I'm seeing what everybody has been saying about the way you feel when you put on this [USA] uniform."

Having won NBA and NCAA titles and countless individual honors, the gold medal was perhaps the only prize that had eluded Johnson. "I'm the kind of guy who likes to play for the moment and who savors things later on, when I've accomplished what I set out to accomplish," he said. "When I'm laying on the beach somewhere, hopefully with the big prize secure, then I can think about what it means to be on the team when NBA players were in the Olympics for the first time."

As delightful for Johnson, however, is the feeling that comes with just being part of a team again—pushing the ball down the court on a fast

break, joking with teammates in the locker room or on the team bus,
playing give-and-take with the media in post-game interview sessions.

"The best thing about this is that I'm one of the boys again," he said,
a gleam in his eye and that luminescent smile on his face. "Being
back—I can't even touch on how I feel. The camaraderie is wonderful,
and how often do you get to be around the best players in the world like
this? I sit in the back of the bus, playing cards… I can't put into words
how I feel being a part of it again."

OUR FIRST TWO WEEKS off went by so fast, I almost didn't know they existed. I spent four days in New Jersey at the Nets' rookie camp and the rest of the time in Detroit, then all of a sudden it's time to head for our pre-Olympic camp in Monte Carlo and the big show in Barcelona.

Since the Basketball Tournament of the Americas, it's been interesting to read articles and watch talk-show discussions about the team, but I'm not sure everyone understands what's going on. Someone wrote that he hoped when we got to Barcelona we would have more discipline, that the players wouldn't wave towels on the bench and look like they were having so much fun because it enhances the image of the "ugly American." Well, I don't see it that way. Guys like that are missing the point. Just because we win, and enjoy winning, doesn't make us ugly Americans.

The other nations knew what they were getting into when they voted to open the Olympics to NBA players. And remember, we voted against that move. The other countries wanted it because they had a vision of how to improve over the long run. Every basketball player, in fact, every serious athlete, knows that his or her performance can only be improved by playing against other competitors who have developed superior skills. Many of

AMERICAN ATHLETES (IN BLUE BLAZERS) PARADE AROUND MONTJUIC STADIUM DURING THE OPENING CEREMONIES OF THE XXV OLYMPIAD.

GOING FOR THE GOLD

our Olympic opponents have voiced the same idea. Sure, they might lose some games by lopsided scores, and, yes, I hope we're going to win a gold medal. That doesn't make us ugly Americans. These games are a measuring stick for the rest of the world, so they can see where they stand and how far they have to go.

Now it's back to work for all of us, although to make conditions more pleasant, the coaches and many of the players brought their families to Europe. There were 11 kids on our charter flight, as young as one-month-old Sean Mullin, and it was fun seeing the kids running—or crawling—up and down the cabin. Some of the guys were playing cards in one of the berths—I think Scottie Pippen and Charles Barkley were the big winners. Across the aisle, in another berth, Larry Bird lay fully extended on a special back-support device for most of the flight. Sitting on a plane really aggravates his injured back, so we're hop-

ing lying flat will alleviate that. His wife, Dinah, and their year-old son, Connor, made the trip with him.

I felt coming over to Europe to practice was important. I've been over here 10, 15 times at least, and I know it takes five or six days to get fully adjusted to the time change. A week in Monte Carlo should have us ready for Barcelona.

We didn't know what to expect when we landed, but even though it was almost midnight there were quite a few people at the airport in Nice. We took a bus to the Loews Monte Carlo Hotel, and when we arrived about 12:30 a.m. there were several hundred people outside to greet us. Their enthusiasm was really something.

Basically, we chose to have our training camp here because we wanted to make this experience as nice as possible for the players, and you can't get much nicer than this! Monte Carlo is absolutely gorgeous. I told C. M. Newton when I was first named coach that he would be shocked at what we would have to do to put this all together. And one of my biggest priorities was to make the week before the Games as enjoyable as we could. Summer is our players' time off, and they want to be with their families. I thought it was only fair to provide this opportunity for the players and their families to enjoy some time together.

Monte Carlo offers plenty of diversions from practicing basketball—maybe too many—between the beaches, the great golf courses, the food, and the casinos. But these guys can handle it, and it's a wonderful trip for their families as well, which works to everyone's benefit. And no, I'm not instituting any curfews. For one thing, I'd have to adhere to them,

KARL AND KAY MALONE PLAY WITH ONE-YEAR-OLD KADEE DURING THE CHARTER FLIGHT TO EUROPE.

CONNOR BIRD, ALSO A YEAR OLD, TAKES A FEED FROM LARRY
WHILE THE CELTICS STAR TRIES TO REST HIS ACHING BACK.

and for another, Jimmy Z's [a popular night spot]
doesn't get going till midnight!

SUNDAY, JULY 19

Even though most of the guys didn't get to sleep till
4 or 5 in the morning, we had a surprisingly good
practice. I thought about giving them the day off
after our long trip but felt it was more important to
get them into the gym for a couple of hours and get
them thinking about basketball again.

To my delight, they picked up right where they
left off in Portland. We didn't have to spend much
time at all reviewing the things that we already
had put in. I called out a play and as they headed
upcourt, Charles turned and said "Oh, yeah, Quick 2.
I remember that." They got very competitive right
away, and the scrimmage became pretty physical. All
in all it was a good workout, although neither Bird

nor Stockton was ready for any contact.

The rest of the day was devoted to R&R. I played
golf at the Monte Carlo Country Club along with
Michael, while others elected to spend time by the
pool. I know a lot of guys hit the casinos at night,
either in the hotel or at the Monte Carlo Sporting
Club. That's the ornate building you see in the
James Bond movies, and it's connected to our hotel
by a roof garden. One guy you won't find in the casinos is Larry Bird. I heard he walked in and asked for
a beer, was told it cost the equivalent of about $7,
and walked right out.

MONDAY, JULY 20

Sometimes the first day back is a high-energy day,
and that's the way it was yesterday. Today was a little
less intense at first, but after awhile they got into it. It
ended up being a good practice, with some of the
guys really talking trash during the scrimmage. It got
physical at the end, which we needed because

"HURRY UP AND WAIT!"—CHRISTIAN LAETTNER (LEFT) IN A PENSIVE MOOD AT NICE AIRPORT. P. J. CARLESIMO (ABOVE) CATCHES UP ON PAPERWORK ON THE WAY TO FRANCE. CHRIS MULLIN'S SON, SEAN, QUIETS DOWN HIS FATHER (BELOW).

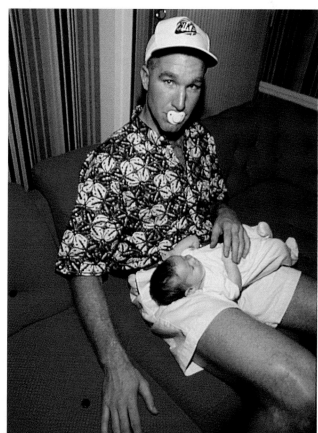

tomorrow we have an exhibition game against the French national team. It will be good for us to see outside competition; there's only so much you can do when you're scrimmaging against your own guys.

Larry Bird practiced in a five-minute scrimmage and looked OK, but I still don't know how much we're going to get out of him before the whole thing is over. John Stockton worked out in the swimming pool and rode a stationery bike, but they tell me he won't be ready to practice until Friday at the earliest.

Speaking of pools, Charles Barkley tells me that after having seen the pool here at our hotel, where some of the women like to go topless, he's thinking of quitting the basketball squad and trying out for the swimming team instead!

Today's my birthday, but I don't think I'm going to do anything special to celebrate. One thing you've

got to understand: When you have a birthday outside of your home country, it doesn't count; not only that, but it reduces your total by one. So I'm back to 60, not up to 62.

Tonight we had a very elegant reception at the hotel, with both Prince Rainier and Prince Albert in attendance. Magic spoke for the team and thanked the princes, as well as the people of Monaco, for making us feel so welcome. He got a big laugh when he said, "I always thought the closest I would get to royalty was playing with Michael Jordan, but this tops that!"

Then they brought a birthday cake to my table, and the band played "Happy Birthday" and every-

EVEN IN POSH MONTE CARLO, PLAYGROUND OF THE RICH AND FAMOUS, FANS LINE UP FOR A GLIMPSE OF AMERICA'S DREAM TEAM.

body sang. Actually, a royal reception isn't a bad way to mark a birthday!

TUESDAY, JULY 21

I read some quotes from David Robinson in the paper this morning, which I thought were very perceptive. He compared our approach to the way the Olympic team prepared in 1988 and said, "There's a big difference in the familiarity of the players. We know each other very well because we play against each other quite a bit. It's easier to come together as a team because you already have a good feel for what guys' strengths and weaknesses are. And you're dealing with more mature players here. On the college level, the coach dominates the game so much, but here the players dominate the game, the flow of play, even the strategy. On the floor, we can change things as we go along. If I see something in the middle, I can tell people how to adjust and they'll respond."

I thought David showed a good understanding of our approach. I've tried to give the players a structure within which to operate on the court, but not to restrain their creativity. I should know it by now, but it never ceases to amaze me how bright they are with regard to basketball and how quickly they pick things up. As coaches at this level, it's up to us to utilize that basketball intelligence and not keep too tight a hold on the reins.

We had a light shootaround in the morning, then played the French national team. This is our only game before Barcelona, and it was the Dream Team's first outing on international soil. Though we were really sloppy at the start, we broke the game open

JOHN STOCKTON FROLICS WITH FIVE-YEAR-OLD SON HOUSTON IN THE POOL AT THE LOEWS MONTE CARLO HOTEL.

after about 10 minutes and eventually won 111–71.

There was one play where Johnson set up Pippen for an acrobatic dunk. I happened to look up at the Royal Box and there was Prince Albert demonstrating for his father how Pippen had dunked it. I heard later that Prince Rainier had asked for me to sit next to him during the game to explain what was going on, and someone had to tell him that my job required me to be on the court with the team. But with Prince Albert next to him, he got all the explanation he needed. Prince Albert is a real sports fan and enjoyed the exhibition immensely.

I wish I could say I enjoyed it as much as he did. We definitely showed the effects of not having played in two weeks. We were very careless, getting called for eight three-second lane violations, turning the ball over too many times, not defending the pick and roll, and not covering the three-point line as we must. But all in all, we got out of this exhibition game what we wanted, which was some work against an outside opponent. And it gives us some things to focus on in practice the rest of the week.

There was a touching moment near the end of the game, after I had already taken Magic out. Some fans started chanting "Ma-gique! Ma-gique!" and pretty soon most of the 3,000 in the stadium were chanting and doing the rhythmic clapping they do over here. Magic got up off the bench and waved to the crowd, with a big smile on his face. I know that kind of support really means a lot to him, and he gets it wherever we go.

WEDNESDAY, JULY 22

I wanted to run the players hard today, because of all the things we did poorly last night. And although we started out a little sluggishly, we ended with a 20-minute scrimmage that was our most competitive since we've been together. Guys were screaming at the referees and talking trash—it got very heated. At one point Magic was upset with the officiating, so he yelled at Michael, "Chicago Stadium! It's like they picked up Chicago Stadium and moved it to Monte Carlo!" And Michael, who is never one to miss a beat when it comes to trash talking, replied, "Hey, man, this is the '90s!" Michael's team ended up winning 40–36.

SOME OF THE DREAM TEAM'S MOST INTENSE ACTION COMES WHEN THE BLUE TEAM SCRIMMAGES AGAINST THE WHITE TEAM DURING PRACTICE.

"I made a big mistake," Magic said later during our media session. "We were up something like 14–2, and I told Michael he'd better get into the show. I don't know why I said it, but Michael just took it over for the next couple of minutes. He is simply the best player in the world. I'm telling myself, 'I've got to stop him,' but in the back of my mind, I know I can't."

Michael does that to everybody. When he gets going, he's unstoppable. You want to know the truth of the matter? In the NBA—forget about international basketball—it should be four against five. But if he beats me in golf like he did yesterday, he will not start in Barcelona!

THURSDAY, JULY 23

Today we worked on trapping out of a zone, which is something we'll use if we want to take the ball out of a particular player's hands. This could be effective against a team that has one really dangerous player. The scrimmage went very well. Jordan's blue team and Johnson's white team tied 48-48 over 20 minutes. I thought our defense was excellent, but our foul shooting needs some work.

I'm a little concerned about the amount of contact, since these scrimmages have been pretty heated, so this is probably the end of our contact work. I certainly don't want to take a chance on getting anyone hurt at this point.

I'm still thinking of using a different starting five for each game. I'm going to try to balance their playing time, but the most important thing will be their responding to their minutes very quickly. I told them that once we get to Barcelona, the hook is in.

JOHN STOCKTON PEDALS A STATIONARY BICYCLE, TRYING TO GET HIS INJURED LEG READY FOR OLYMPIC ACTION.

If somebody isn't playing well, he's going to sit and his minutes will go to someone else. But that's not going to be a problem. I like where this team is. Their focus is good; they know what they have to do. Plus we're now moving to Barcelona, so their late-night activities should be curtailed somewhat and maybe they'll get some sleep for a change!

Speaking of late-night activities, I heard Magic was a big winner in the casino and when he got up to cash in his chips, everybody cheered and he blew kisses to the crowd and it was quite a scene. Then I understand that the cashier, who obviously doesn't follow basketball, mistook Magic for another U.S. player and tried to get him to pay off some markers!

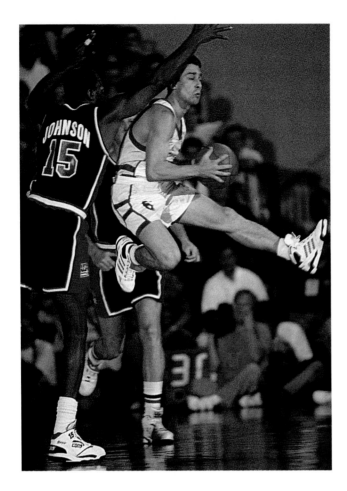

AT 6-9, "MA-GIQUE" JOHNSON PROVES TOO MUCH OF AN OBSTACLE FOR THE FRENCH NATIONAL TEAM TO OVERCOME DURING AN EXHIBITION GAME.

FRIDAY, JULY 24

Monte Carlo has been as close as you can get to perfection as a place to bring a group like this together. It is truly an idyllic setting, and the atmosphere really took the edge off going back to work. We got exactly what we wanted out of the week, which was to get them back to focusing on basketball while still making it an enjoyable experience for them and their families.

Things are going to get a little more interesting in Barcelona, and I don't necessarily mean that in a positive way. Until this point we've been able to control everything—food, hotel, gyms, all those kinds of things. Now we're going into the Olympics, a FIBA competition, where they're going to be in control and we're going to have to adapt. We talked about that at practice today—we're going to have to show a lot more patience at times.

One of the reasons we picked a site other than Barcelona for the training camp was that we felt three weeks in one place would be too much. I think two weeks is going to be tough. Our guys are used to moving on to another city every couple of days. In our league we say that sometimes your feet never hit the ground, but it's a way of life you learn to like. I heard Charles Barkley say on the team bus, "Can't we play doubleheaders, wrap this up in a week, and get out of Dodge? I want to get home to Alabama."

Our flight was only about an hour and a half, but we landed at Reus Airport, which is about an hour from the regular Barcelona airport. We planned this because there were about 30 heads of state scheduled to come into the Barcelona airport today, with the airport closing down 10 or 15 minutes for each one. We thought it might take us two hours or more to get through the airport, and we didn't want to go through that. The tradeoff is that we had a longer bus ride into the city, but I think it was the lesser of two evils because this way we were able to get tremendous security, a full police escort with a helicopter overhead, and we got to the hotel without incident.

Before settling in, the players and coaches went to the Olympic Village to get our accreditation, and something happened that gives you an idea of what sets this team apart. We were fortunate in that we got our credentials rather quickly—P. J. Carlesimo had warned me that sometimes it takes up to five hours, but they did an amazing job getting us through. Then some of the volunteers started to come over for autographs, but they had to put a stop to that because too many were leaving their posts.

Finally we had to walk about two blocks to our bus, and along the way many of the athletes came out on their balconies and there was a lot of screaming and cheering. Then there was a big group of media, surrounding us and pushing and shoving. Charlie Vincent, who writes for the *Detroit Free Press*, said even he was impressed because it was really a wild scene and we had to get on the bus just for safety's sake. It got very active and a little bit scary, and it underscored the nature of the security risk involved with these players wherever we travel. People think we can just go around normally, but we can't.

That's the thing to keep in mind whenever any-

AFTER THE TEAMS POSE FOR A PRE-GAME PHOTO (ABOVE), CHARLES BARKLEY (NO. 14, BELOW) DRIVES FOR TWO OF HIS 21 POINTS AS THE U.S. DEFEATS THE FRENCH NATIONAL TEAM 111–71 IN ITS LONE OLYMPIC TUNEUP.

body asks how come we stayed at a hotel and not in the Village. There's no understanding of the security that these players need, not just from the public but from the media and guests and even other athletes. They are seen all over the world on TV, and they are bigger than life. They can't blend into a crowd. It's

like traveling with a dozen major rock stars when you're with this team. It would be chaos if we didn't control it as best we could.

NBA Commissioner David J. Stern brought up a good point in this matter when he said, "Our players have been on the road and away from their families for a large measure of time between October and the middle of June. They were told by USA Basketball that it would be made as easy as possible for them, in terms of spending time with their families, their children, and at the same time competing in the Olympics. And so we did for them what the track and

field stars have done in the past, the tennis professionals, and other people. It really wasn't an issue." Considering the fame of our players, we had to protect them and their families.

While we were on the bus, the players spotted the women's gymnastics team outside. They asked these young ladies to come on the bus and gave them autographs and posed for pictures. The gymnasts were really excited. Our guys applauded them as they got off the bus because they know how hard they have to train and all that goes into what they do, and I thought that was a very nice touch.

SATURDAY, JULY 25

Today we went to the main press center for a news conference before more than 1,000 members of the media. Then we practiced for an hour in preparation for our opening game tomorrow against Angola. The news conference was difficult because there were so many people in attendance. It was rather impersonal, and many of the questions were those we had heard so many times before.

The business about the Village came up, which I've already addressed, and I tried to make another point by having Patrick Ewing and David Robinson stand up. I asked whether there were any beds in the Village in which they could fit, which is something people often overlook. I also said that in all the time this team has been together in La Jolla, Portland, and Monte Carlo, our experience yesterday with the stampede of athletes and media was the most frightening. Magic Johnson, who is used to dealing with crowds, made a point of saying, "We're here in body and in spirit, we gave up our summer to be here, we're having the times of our lives, and we share the

TRAINER ED LACERTE (IN WHITE SHIRT, FACING CAMERA) PUTS THE TEAM THROUGH STRETCHING EXERCISES AT THE START OF EACH PRACTICE IN MONTE CARLO. FOR LARRY BIRD (SEE NEXT PAGE), THE BAD BACK THAT WOULD FORCE HIS EARLY RETIREMENT LIMITS HIS PRACTICE TIME.

Olympic spirit just like any other athlete. We'll be in the Olympic Village; we just won't be living there. But if what happened yesterday happens again, we'll just have to pull back because it got a little crazy with everybody running over."

They asked about professionalism in the Olympics, which I think is another moot point. Look at all the endorsements a guy like Carl Lewis has—you can't go two blocks in this city without seeing his face on some billboard. And as Magic said, "For years other countries sent guys who were getting paid and nobody said anything about it. But when we do it, all of a sudden it's a big deal? Just treat us the same as everyone else."

TAKING TO THE LINKS ARE (ABOVE, LEFT TO RIGHT) ROD THORN, MICHAEL JORDAN, CHUCK DALY, P. J. CARLESIMO. THE "DREAM KIDS" (BELOW) COME IN ALL SIZES AND MAKE THE TRIP TO BARCELONA VERY MUCH A FAMILY AFFAIR.

Other countries send their best players—should we have to send our second-best just because our best are so good? Since when is excellence a disqualifying factor in athletics? With that logic, Cuba shouldn't send its boxers, China's divers would have to stay home, and so forth. All world champions or previous Olympic champions would be ineligible since they have already proven themselves to be too good. Obviously that's ridiculous, so, as Magic says, just treat us the same as everyone else.

As usual when the media is around, Charles stole the show. About our first opponent he said, "I don't know anything about Angola, but Angola's in trouble!" When asked about the United States's controversial loss to the Soviet Union in 1972, he said, "I had just flunked my entrance exam to kindergarten so I don't know much about that." And about using NBA players in the Olympics he said, "I don't understand why it's such a big deal now, when other countries have used pros for years. Why don't they just take their…whipping like men and go home?" Leave it to Charles to lay things on the line!

Someone asked me if I thought about trying to put a muzzle on Charles, and my answer was no. Even if I tried, it wouldn't do any good. We've talked about dealing with the media and the public, of course, but Charles is his own man and you have to respect him for that, even if you feel he could be a little more discreet at times. He's intelligent and often makes valid points, but every once in awhile he'll say something off the top of his head that he doesn't mean in a harmful or negative way, but which nonetheless offends some people. That's where he should think of the

CLYDE DREXLER (ABOVE) CATCHES UP ON HIS READING AS THE TEAM BUS CIRCLES BARCELONA'S STATUE OF CHRISTOPHER COLUMBUS.

consequences of his remarks before he speaks. He's a colorful character, I'll say that. I admire the way he plays, and any coach who has had him will tell you he always gives his best effort. Nonetheless, I'm happy I'm only coaching him for seven weeks!

Eight of our players—all except for Larry Bird, who has a bad back, and Chris Mullin, Patrick Ewing, and Michael Jordan, who marched in 1984—joined the four coaches in participating in tonight's Opening Ceremonies, so we were very well represented. One of our photographers gave Charles Barkley a camera, and he was snapping away like crazy. When we marched into the stadium they put us in the front alongside the track, and when each country came by some of its athletes would break ranks and try to get autographs or exchange high fives or have pictures taken with our guys. It was all in good fun and good spirit, but it became difficult to shield ourselves from it, particularly Magic. He is really a worldwide celebrity. In fact, I was shocked at how recognized he is around the world.

It was a very emotional night. I was standing with

Magic and he felt the same way. Later he said, "Marching with all those athletes was one of the greatest days of my life—the feeling I felt, I've never reached that high." I thought the lighting of the torch with an arrow shot by archer Antonio Rebollo was very dramatic, and the magnificent opera singers were fabulous. It was, all in all, a spectacular show.

SUNDAY, JULY 26

Tonight we finally played our first game, beating a much smaller Angolan team 116–48. We shot 64 percent and outscored them 46–1 in one stretch of the first half, which is kind of amazing. Charles was our leading scorer with 24 points, and Magic had 10 assists. Someone from the Angolan delegation had said he thought they didn't play any defense in the NBA, and of course we in the league know how tough these people can be. So we dropped the word

to the players, and they went out and did a good job. We had 30 steals, which is a big number, and we held them to 25 percent shooting.

It was good to work under game conditions, see the arena, learn about the traffic, get used to the whole scene. We know we may have a close game down the line—maybe tomorrow, when we play Croatia—so this will help us be prepared.

The support group we have from security to get us around has been fantastic. We have the same motorcycle cop we had in Monte Carlo leading our motorcade and, I'll tell you, it was a little scary sitting in the front seat of the bus. I saw too many close calls! But they've done a great job getting us to and from places.

AMERICA'S DREAM TEAM ANSWERS QUESTIONS FROM SOME OF THE MORE THAN 1,000 MEDIA MEMBERS WHO FILL THE AUDITORIUM AT THE MAIN PRESS CENTER.

We're staying at the Ambassador, a new hotel on a small side street off Las Ramblas, which is Barcelona's main tree-lined promenade. The sights on Las Ramblas are something, from the mimes working the street to the stands that sell live birds and animals to the crowds from all different countries who are here for the Olympics. One reason the people who planned our trip, including Horace Balmer, the NBA's vice president and director of security, wanted this hotel was because they knew they could secure it, and they really have. Nobody gets in without a special photo ID issued by USA Basketball, and there are guards all around, inside and outside the building, with a sharpshooter on the roof around the clock. They've done a nice job with the hotel, which just opened last month. It's typically European, with smaller rooms than we're accustomed to, but very nice—and air conditioned, which is a blessing. Why they don't air condition the Olympic Village is beyond me. Don't the athletes deserve it?

I had gotten a card earlier in the day from one of the Chrysler security people telling me that Lee Iacocca was staying across the street at the Meridien Hotel and inviting me to stop by, since they couldn't get into our hotel. So when Lenny Wilkens and I came back from scouting Croatia at the arena, we went over to the Meridien and spent a really enjoyable half-hour with Lee and his wife, Darien. It's amazing that while I'd been in Detroit for nine years and never met the man, here we were having drinks together halfway around the world. I really enjoyed meeting him. I can see why he's successful: he's so dynamic.

MONDAY, JULY 27

I only let Michael Jordan play nine holes today because I wanted him to be ready for our game tonight against Croatia, which so many people are

EVEN IN BARCELONA, MICHAEL JORDAN IS LARGER THAN LIFE—ESPECIALLY IN THIS SEVEN-STORY BILLBOARD FROM HIS FAVORITE SNEAKER COMPANY.

picking to win a medal. As it turned out, maybe not letting him play 18 left him too hyper, because he did not shoot the ball well (9 for 22). I guess he needs to play a full round of golf in order to get calmed down for basketball!

Our entire group sensed that this game might be tougher than the ones we've played so far, because Croatia was one of the best teams in the European qualifying tournament. Also, their star is Toni Kukoc, whose rights are owned by the Chicago Bulls and who has a big contract to play in Italy. I know

Michael and Scottie wanted to test him and see what he's all about. To be perfectly honest, I decided to start Scottie not because of the Bulls incident (Pippen was upset when the Bulls delayed renegotiating his contract when they first tried to sign Kukoc), but because I felt we needed great defensive intensity from the start, and Scottie is one of our

A FLAG-WAVING KARL MALONE (CENTER, BELOW) IS ONE OF EIGHT PLAYERS (TOP, OPPOSITE PAGE) MARCHING IN THE OPENING CEREMONIES, WHICH INCLUDED A SPECTACULAR MEDITERRANEAN PAGEANT (PAGES 194-5). BARCELONA AT NIGHT (BOTTOM, OPPOSITE PAGE) WAS AGLOW WITH LIGHTS.

best defensive players. A year ago I told Rod Thorn that I sensed we would need Scottie to play against Kukoc if we ever met in the Olympics, because Pippen has the size and quickness to defend against a guy who plays the point forward the way Kukoc does. It turned out to be somewhat prophetic because this game was Scottie's defensive showcase.

Even though we lost Magic to a hamstring injury after only 8 1/2 minutes, we were leading 19–8 at that point and stretched it to 42–18 on a great breakaway slam by Scottie that brought everyone up off the bench. Croatia came within 15 in the second half, but we stayed in control because of our defense, even though we didn't shoot all that well, and won 103–70. Michael scored 21 and Charles had 20, while Kukoc had only 4 points on 2-for-11 shooting. He later said, "I never saw that kind of defense before. From the first moment, Scottie was all over me." But Kukoc's a very good basketball player. As he plays against us more and as he gets physically stronger, he'll get better. He's definitely an NBA player, but I think Scottie showed him some things tonight.

How seriously did we take this game? In the morning we had one of our first shootarounds, and even though it was about 95 degrees in the practice facility, we walked through several of Croatia's plays to make sure our guys were familiar with them. We haven't done that for anyone else. And when we went to the arena tonight, you could sense on the bus and in the locker room that this one was for real.

Magic's injury is a concern, although the MRI on his left knee was negative and it now appears to be a strained hamstring. We're already thin at point guard,

because John Stockton hasn't been able to play or practice since the second game of the Tournament of the Americas. Scottie and Michael may have to do the job at that position for the next game or two.

TUESDAY, JULY 28

I gave everybody the day off today. It's our first day off in a while, and we need to get away from each other and spend the day with our families or playing golf or whatever.

The atmosphere at last night's game was something special. They have five rows behind the team benches set aside for officials and players from other

basketball teams who are not competing that day, and most nights those rows are pretty empty. Last night they were packed with players from just about every team, men's and women's, in the Olympics. They all had their cameras and video cameras and were shooting away. I went out about 25 minutes early and just sat there and absorbed the electricity. There was something different about that game. I got a sense that the arena was waiting to explode if Croatia had stayed in the game longer. People were hoping to be able to root for the giant-killer. As the saying goes, everybody likes to cheer for David and

not Goliath. That's why it was important that we came out with the intensity that we did, especially on defense. Again I say, we are the team that can defeat us. Our attitude, if we get overconfident, could be our biggest threat. If we continue to play defense and run, people are not going to be able to stop us.

WEDNESDAY, JULY 29

Another controversy has arisen, this time regarding the uniform our players would wear if we win the gold medal. The official USOC ceremony uniform is made by Reebok, while many of our players are under contract to Nike or other companies and are reluctant to advertise a competitor. I can see both sides. The USOC has a major sponsor who is counting on the exposure it receives at a high-profile medal ceremony [mandatory for all 650 athletes]. Our individuals have major contracts of their own, however, and you have to respect them for trying to live up to their agreements. Maybe they'll work out a compromise to get through this year and then try to come up with a solution down the road.

Maintaining the proper focus throughout this tournament is going to be tough because of the length of time involved and because of all the distractions. It's hard to stay intense for two weeks, even for our people, who are used to challenges at the highest level.

Tonight we beat Germany much more easily than I expected, 111–68, in a game that was never in doubt. I had been concerned because we were so sky-high

CHARLES BARKLEY'S ROUGH PLAY AGAINST ANGOLA (LEFT) CAUSES A STIR, BUT IT'S MAGIC JOHNSON (RIGHT) WHO HAS TO BE HELPED OFF THE FLOOR WITH A HAMSTRING INJURY DURING THE GAME AGAINST CROATIA.

for Croatia and then we'd had our first day off. I didn't know how they would come back. And injuries had left us short-handed at guard, where Michael Jordan and Scottie Pippen had to play the point. But everything went "according to Hoyle," as they say.

When this group gets in the locker room, their leadership qualities emerge. They're all leaders on their teams, all vocal guys, and you could see that in the locker room tonight. Magic was very vocal even though he wasn't going to play. Barkley was vocal. Everybody got each other up for the game, and we went out and got the job done. We played good defense, jumped ahead 28–8 after the first 12 minutes, and by halftime it was 58–23. Michael had a fine all-around game with 15 points, 12 assists, and no turnovers, and Larry Bird had his best game of the

BRANFORD MARSALIS (LEFT) AND DAVID ROBINSON COMPARE NOTES DURING A MUSICAL INTERLUDE ON THE ROOF OF THE HOTEL AMBASSADOR.

summer with 19 points and some great passing.

THURSDAY, JULY 30

We're going to stay with the formula that worked well the past two days. Today's a day off, then we play Brazil on Friday night. We'll have a team meeting before the game. I don't think our team is going to have any trouble getting up for this game, as Charles Barkley explained in *USA Today*: "We want them bad. It goes back to Portland, when they said they were going to be our worst nightmare. They said we weren't taking this seriously and all we were doing was playing golf and goofing around. Well, we'll see Friday. We'll see who is whose nightmare. I can't wait. They're in trouble—and I think they know it."

Most of our players, along with coaches Lenny Wilkens and Mike Krzyzewski, went to watch the

U.S. women's team beat Czechoslovakia 111–55. I'm glad our guys showed that kind of support for the women's team because they've been very supportive of us. It's nice we could reciprocate.

Our players have been going to many different events. Magic Johnson went to gymnastics tonight, Karl Malone to boxing, Larry Bird to baseball, and Charles Barkley to swimming. Charles really spoke for the whole team when he said, "It's important to show all the American athletes we're behind them. We're all in the same boat, and I want to show my support for the American athletes whenever I can."

FRIDAY, JULY 31

Brazil tried to run with us and kept pace for the first few minutes. Then they seemed to tire. We went from 17–15 to 34–21 very quickly and were never in trouble. We won 127–83 to raise our record to 4–0 and clinch first place in Pool A of the round-robin competition. The 127 points were the most ever scored by a U.S. Olympic team, and if Brazil had stayed competitive longer we might have hit 150. Charles Barkley had another big game, scoring 30 points, on 12 for 14 from the field, and also doing a great job defensively against Brazil's star, Oscar Schmidt. The leading scorer in the Italian League last year at 38 ppg., Oscar (who can "score the ball," as they say over here) shot just 8 for 25. He got many of his 24 points long after the outcome was determined.

We seem to have hit a lull, with the scores being as one-sided as they are. Plus tonight was our first late game, starting at 10:30 p.m., so I suspected we might not come out very sharp. And I was right. Brazil ran the ball back at us and was not afraid to play an up tempo, but ultimately that wore them down and they were unable to stay competitive.

Michael Jordan came down with a touch of the flu before the game, which put us in a really tough position at guard, with Magic Johnson and John Stockton on the sidelines. Scottie Pippen had to play more minutes (27) than normal, and we used Chris Mullin and Clyde Drexler back in that area as well.

Our games have come so easily that the mental part, the lack of sharpness, has become a little disturbing to the coaching staff. What we do about it, though, I'm not sure. Maybe we'll get a lift if Magic will come back Sunday. Maybe that will stir things up. We've talked about holding a practice on Monday, but that's a hard sell because the margins of victory have been so large.

I'm also a little concerned about conditioning, with no practices. One thing that happens when you bring an entourage like we have at the hotel—wives, girlfriends, children, and others—is that guys who otherwise might be working out, instead spend their time doing other things. That's why most NBA clubs do not allow families to travel with the team during the course of the season, because it can become a distraction. But we've been able to handle all the mental aspects of the competition thus far, and I hope it continues.

When we got back to the hotel after the game we had a Chinese buffet instead of the hotel's regular food (or the burgers, chicken, and pizza we've been having brought in from nearby fast food places). So here we are, a bunch of Americans eating Chinese food in Barcelona at 2 a.m. after having played an Olympic basketball game. Sometimes you have to step back and marvel at it all!

SATURDAY, AUGUST 1

Some of the guys went to a club called Bonasport and worked out, which should help their conditioning. Then a group went over to the Olympic Village and walked around among the other athletes, and guys went to various events tonight. Track and field was the hot ticket, with the finals of the men's and women's 100-meter dash, and my wife, Terry, and I went along with several of our players.

On our way back to the hotel, we found that many streets were blocked off because they were running the women's Olympic marathon through the city. Our bus got stopped for 10 or 15 minutes, and Chris

AFTER PRACTICE, PATRICK EWING ICES DOWN HIS SORE KNEES ON THE TEAM BUS.

CLYDE DREXLER (IN RED SHIRT) AND KARL MALONE SHOW
THEIR SUPPORT TO MEMBERS OF THE WOMEN'S TEAM.

Mullin and John Stockton decided to get off and take the subway back. Then Magic and some more players decided to do the same thing, and our security guys started to get a little worried. So they coaxed them back onto the bus, and ultimately we got through the roadblock and beat the subway group back to the hotel. But Horace Balmer and I were concerned because the security people are very serious about protecting the team, and they don't like any deviations from the plan.

SUNDAY, AUGUST 2

Before the game against Spain tonight, Magic indicated he'd like to play about five minutes and Stockton said the same, so for the first time since our initial game in Portland we had all 12 players available. Of course, this creates a problem for me in terms of distributing playing time. It's impossible to give each of the 12 guys the minutes he wants, but I managed to work John into the rotation in the first half. With Magic, I decided to have him warm up at half time and let him start the second half and get

some minutes that way. Neither one looked very mobile, although I was happy to get them both back in action. It was nice to see John hit a three-pointer and get in the Olympic scorebook.

The home crowd was really spirited for this game, even though Spain has not done well in this tournament. The game fell into the same pattern as the rest of our games. We got off to a pretty good lead in the first half and put it out of reach early. Then we got a little careless and kind of rode with the score for about 10 minutes before our talent and depth took over again and we pulled away to a 122–81 win.

MONDAY, AUGUST 3

The uniform controversy seems to have been resolved. Michael Jordan, who was thrust into the forefront of it, said he'd leave it to Dave Gavitt to work out a solution. Dave has satisfied the USOC by promising that all our players will appear on the medal stand in the official Reebok-made uniform, although it may be worn in such a way that the company logo will not be visible. I'm going to let somebody else in our group worry about how to pin the uniforms so the logo is covered; I've got enough other things on my mind.

We practiced for about an hour today. I wanted to work on some ballhandling and shooting and get the guys a little extra running and work on the court, and I think it was useful.

One thing about Charles Barkley: he doesn't miss a trick. When we started our lay-up drills, Charles noticed that Clyde Drexler was wearing two right sneakers. Clyde evidently had forgotten his left sneaker but decided to try to get through practice because he didn't want to face the razzing he'd get from the guys. But Charles wasn't going to let Clyde off easily and said, "I know you Portland guys are dumb, but Jerome Kersey wouldn't come to practice with two right shoes!" Everybody cracked up. Fortunately Larry Bird had an extra pair of shoes with him and Clyde borrowed his left, but it looked strange as he finished practice wearing different brands of shoes.

With the win over Spain, we completed our play in the preliminary round as the only team with a 5–0 record. But I tried to impress upon the players that we're really back to 0–0 now. All we've done thus far doesn't mean a thing because if we lose a game now we're out of the tournament. We need to try to re-focus, and it's not easy, especially because all the time spent together in one place is sort of wearing on everyone at this point. A writer asked me, in view of our one-sided victories, whether I still was concerned. I said, "Sure, I'm concerned. Overwhelming favorites are always being set up to be knocked off. I've seen it happen too many times: Villanova-Georgetown, Duke-UNLV, the

1980 Soviet hockey team that beat the NHL clubs before losing to the U.S. Olympians. Anything can happen, so sure, I'm concerned."

We will be playing Puerto Rico in the quarterfinals on Tuesday night, and they looked good in beating the Unified Team before our game last night. They are playing with a lot more confidence than when we

PATRICK EWING SETS UP A FORMIDABLE ROADBLOCK DURING THE U.S. TEAM'S 122–81 WIN OVER SPAIN.

faced them in Portland. However, we did beat them by 38 points, so where will our heads be?

TUESDAY, AUGUST 4

We scored the first 17 points of the game, then got semi-bored and Puerto Rico scored the next 13. This time we got good production from an unusual lineup I used late in the first half because of foul trouble. We had Magic and Stockton playing together along with Pippen, Mullin, and Laettner, all good shooters and ballhandlers. We got open shots and started hitting them, and by half time we led 67–40. Puerto Rico hung around for awhile by going to a matchup zone that didn't allow us to run, but we ended up

MICHAEL JORDAN (BELOW) OUTJUMPS PUERTO RICO'S JOSE ORTIZ FOR A REBOUND DURING THE 115–77 QUARTERFINAL VICTORY. DURING AN OFF-DAY, JORDAN VISITED MONTJUIC STADIUM (RIGHT) FOR A LOOK AT THE OLYMPIC FLAME.

beating them 115–77. The 38-point margin was the same we had over them in Portland.

This game showed one reason the NBA doesn't allow zone defenses, because Michael Jordan and some of the others were unable to run and slash to the basket the way they like. Zones lead to jump-shooting contests, and that keeps the players from being able to use all of their skills. The fans want to see players perform to the max.

We won't practice Wednesday. We didn't arrive back at the hotel until 1 a.m., and then everybody started eating and hanging out. There's no way to get to sleep until at least 3 a.m., so a practice later is a futile effort. It's better to have a shootaround on game day, which we will do Thursday.

WEDNESDAY, AUGUST 5

This turned out to be a rough day for USA Basketball. Our women's team lost to the Unified Team 79–73 in the semifinals, so the best they can do is a bronze medal. I know they must feel devastated. Also, Lenny Wilkens tore his Achilles tendon in a pickup basketball game between USAB officials and Spanish security personnel and will have to undergo surgery when we get back to the States next week. I told his wife, Marilyn, he should have stuck to playing golf. It's a lot safer!

We expected to play Lithuania in either the semifinals or finals, and, as it turns out, it will be the semifinals. They're a tough team (although the tie-dyed warmup shirts they got from the Grateful Dead in their fund-raising drive are not exactly my style). Sarunas Marciulionis, who plays for the Golden State

Warriors, is an excellent scorer who drives to the basket and gets to the foul line 10 or more times every game. Arvydas Sabonis is 7–3 and perhaps the best-known center outside the NBA, having played for the Soviet national team for almost a decade. Although he's slowed because of Achilles tendon injuries, Sabonis remains a good passer and rebounder, and when he catches the ball down low, he's almost impossible to stop. Plus they have some other guys who can shoot the three-pointer, so they're a very capable team.

Focus is the No. 1 reason for our game-day shootarounds: to get the players to focus on Lithuania, in this case. The actual physical part isn't as important. We will make them aware of what the Lithuanians try to do and make some definite plans defensively. This should be an interesting game, and I hope our people respond.

THURSDAY, AUGUST 6

I've been sleeping fairly well up until last night, but I was concerned about this particular game. I thought Lithuania would be an extremely dangerous opponent, and I expressed my concerns to the team in our shootaround. They were very attentive, and, while we only worked for about 45 minutes, it was a valuable session.

When we got to the game it was obvious we were really ready to play. We started a very strong defensive unit with Pippen at one of the forwards and held them scoreless for the first three minutes as we jumped in front 11–0. Then Scottie hurt his hand, but Chris Mullin came in and probably had his best

game, at least defensively. Michael did an excellent job on Marciulionis, and Sabonis had a tough night shooting. With those two under control we were able to win much more easily than I expected, 127–76. I had anticipated a much closer game, but we were into it defensively. And nine of our players scored in double figures, which is remarkable in a 40-minute game.

Marciulionis had been a dominant force in most of Lithuania's games, but Michael never let him get going. He shot just 6 for 17, made 7 turnovers, and only got to the foul line 6 times, which is very low for him. Michael played 27 holes today and had a good night's sleep, so maybe that's the key combination!

Barkley, in a column he's doing with Dave DuPree of *USA Today*, mentioned that the women's team's loss served as a reminder to the men that anything can happen. The women had won their first two games by margins similar to ours, then were beaten in their semifinal outing. Perhaps that reminder was what it took, because this was probably our best all-around game of the tournament.

FRIDAY, AUGUST 7

Finally we're just one win away from our goal, the gold medal. We're taking another day off and will have a shootaround tomorrow. If the gold medal is not enough of an incentive for Saturday's game, I don't know what is. That's the reason we're all here and why we've given up most of our summer.

Some of our players watched the women's team beat Cuba to earn a bronze medal. I'm glad they'll be going home with an Olympic medal, even though it's not the medal they wanted as their first choice.

I watched yesterday's semifinal between the Unified Team and Croatia and was surprised when the Unified Team missed five one-and-ones down the stretch and let Croatia come from behind and win 75–74. Frankly, I had been hoping the Unified Team would win, because it's easier to play a new team than one you've already faced in a tournament. We were so motivated when we played Croatia the first time and we won by 33, so there might be a tendency to let down a bit. Actually, I thought they played us pretty well the first time. I expect Kukoc will have a much better game, and I think Petrovic will be himself. They should be a little looser, and it could be a very interesting game.

MICHAEL JORDAN PICKS UP A LOOSE BALL AND HEADS UPCOURT IN THE 127–76 SEMIFINAL VICTORY OVER LITHUANIA.

SATURDAY, AUGUST 8

As a coach, you look for anything you can find to motivate your team. You never know what is going to give you that little edge that can make all the difference in the world.

I received a note under my door from Dick Ebersol of NBC saying that they had a tape available of a 12-minute piece they aired last night about the U.S. team's controversial loss to the Soviet Union in the 1972 Olympics. P. J. and I looked at it on P. J.'s portable VCR, and we thought it would be worthwhile. When we went to our regular pre-game meeting at 7:30, however, for some reason we were unable to play the tape on the machine at the session. So we looked at a scouting tape of Croatia put together by Pete Skorich of the Detroit Pistons, who did all our video work, and P. J., who did our scout-

ing. We took the NBC tape to the arena and showed it in the locker room before the game, and everyone was very attentive. I thought it was very useful in terms of reminding the players what could happen. We didn't want to let the gold slip away now.

Nevertheless, after all that, we came out flat. We weren't as aggressive defensively as we had to be. We let them stay close, and then they went on a run and actually pulled ahead 25–23, the only time in the entire Olympics we trailed after the opening minutes. In an NBA game I'd have called a time-out at that point, but I knew Croatia already had asked for one so I waited. Besides, I had set two goals before the Olympics—never to call a time-out, because I didn't want to give other teams a breather, and never to stand up during a game. I did stand up a few times to talk to the referees, but this was the only instance I seriously thought about a time-out. Then Charles nailed a three-pointer and set up Clyde for a basket, and we were back in front before the time-out was called.

In the final game on the road, players are already packed and on their way home before you start. The result is usually less-than-stellar. I told them to get

their heads back into this game because we still had something to accomplish.

From the point where we trailed 25–23, we outscored Croatia 27–13 over a period of seven minutes to take a 14-point lead, which was the margin at half time. Then we started the second half with an 11–2 run, Michael getting six of those points. We soon had another 11–0 run to blow the game wide open.

As the final seconds ticked away, the scoreboard read USA 117, Croatia 85. We had accomplished what we had set out to do, and it was a great feeling. We had won the gold medal.

These twelve superstars had come together to form a super team. Both on and off the court, they represented the United States in the best of Olympic traditions. They were truly what their nickname promised—a Dream Team.

MAGIC JOHNSON DISHES ONE OF HIS NO-LOOK PASSES TO PATRICK EWING (PARTIALLY OBSCURED BY CROATIA'S DRAZEN PETROVIC, NO. 4) DURING THE GOLD MEDAL GAME.

BEYOND BARCELONA

W ILL THERE EVER BE another Dream Team?

No. Because this was the first Olympic team to include NBA stars, it will always remain unique. Larry Bird and Magic Johnson have been on international TV and played in the NBA Finals for decades and are acknowledged to be among the greatest players of all time. Michael Jordan, in his prime, is another of the all-time greats. Add to this mix the Malones, the Barkleys, the Ewings, the Robinsons, all the relative newcomers to the scene, and the roster was truly remarkable.

I don't think that can ever happen again, particularly from the public relations standpoint. While some of these people may be able to play in the next Olympics, there will be a whole new group of great players. The next team might include people like Shaquille O'Neal, Alonzo Mourning, Harold Miner, Jimmy Jackson, Larry Johnson, Kendall Gill, Derrick Coleman, or some people who are still in college right now. But I doubt whether, by 1996, those people will have established the reputations that the Dream Team players had. And unless these young stars win NBA titles or move to All-Star status year in and year out, they won't be on the same level as the Dream Team players. It's true that because the Olympics will be in the USA in 1996, in Atlanta, there will be quite a bit of hype, but I doubt the U.S. team will ever be the same as this one.

AMERICA'S DREAM TEAM LEFT ITS MARK ON BARCELONA AND THE OLYMPIC GAMES.

SARUNAS MARCIULIONIS (NO. 13) OF THE GOLDEN STATE WARRIORS LED LITHUANIA TO THE BRONZE MEDAL.

In his news conference at the conclusion of the Olympics, Juan Antonio Samaranch, president of the International Olympic Committee, said, "The Dream Team brought the basketball competition to a new level." I hope that is the way people will remember our participation, because that was what FIBA officials had in mind when they invited us.

Had the people who criticized our presence in the Olympics been involved with us on a day-to-day basis, they would have had a better understanding of what an impact this team made, not only on basketball but on the entire Olympic Games. There were many great events and great athletes in Barcelona, but I think the Dream Team captured the imagination of everyone at the Olympics in a special way. Whether that's good or bad, I don't know. It might change the face of the Games. A U.S. hockey "Dream Team" might go to the 1994 Winter Olympics, and

Samaranch has called for the inclusion of professionals in baseball, soccer, and cycling in the next Summer Olympics. But if the Games are meant to be the ultimate athletic competition, the best athletes in each sport should be permitted to participate.

I know many countries will take a long look at what the United States did with this team in terms of advertising dollars, merchandising, sponsorships, and so on. Some might say, "We're not interested in that," and that's fine for them. But to say the Olympics are for amateur athletes is being rather naive. And I don't mean just the Carl Lewis billboards that were all over Barcelona, or the big-name tennis players who dominated that competition. Each Spanish individual gold medal winner will receive a $1 million pension at age 50, and I read that the Spanish government had spent $120 million on coaches and ath-

THE LITHUANIAN TEAM'S BAY-AREA CONNECTION WAS UNDERSCORED BY THE DISTINCTIVE TIE-DYED SHORTS AND T-SHIRTS CONTRIBUTED BY THE ROCK BAND, THE GRATEFUL DEAD.

DETLEF SCHREMPF
OF THE INDIANA
PACERS HELPED
GERMANY TO A 7TH-
PLACE FINISH, ITS
HIGHEST EVER.

letes over the past four years in order to improve its performance in the 1992 Olympics—an investment that paid off in 20 medals, including 13 gold, for the host country. I think many countries in the Olympics will realize the impact money can have, in so many ways.

One thing I found very interesting was the reaction we received from the teams we played. These are all competitive athletes who came to Barcelona to win, so there may have been some resentment by some individuals. But for the vast majority, I think they were pleased at having the chance to play against us, against a team of this caliber.

That was certainly the case with everything I heard and read, both in Barcelona and Portland. I believe they enjoyed the experience. I know Arturas Karnisovas of Lithuania, who plays for P. J. Carlesimo at Seton Hall, will never forget it. "When I was playing," he said, "I told our manager to take a few pictures of me guarding Barkley. Then, when I was on the bench, I decided to take a few more shots. Just one roll. These are the stars from the stars. They exceeded my expectations."

The players on the Dream Team are people that you can't help but admire. I didn't know most of our players, except on a 'hello' basis and from having competed against them, before we came together in La Jolla. When I got them all together and watched what they were capable of doing, it was a little frightening. You easily can be awed by it. I had to grow into relationships with this team and with these other coaches, and the same thing happened with the teams that played against us. They knew they were playing the best in the world. Down deep I don't think they felt they could win, but they respected us, and they enjoyed the competition. They'll go home and for the rest of their lives be able to tell their kids, "I played against Michael Jordan and Magic Johnson and Larry Bird." And the more they play against our best players, the more confident they're going to get.

Alexander Gomelsky, who coached the Soviet Union to the gold medal in 1988 and who is known as the father of basketball in his homeland, is among those with what I call a worldwide vision of the sport. I frequently saw him on the sidelines watching our games. "The way the NBA stars play is dream basketball," he said once. "That is right, it is not journalistic hype. This is a nice teacher of basketball. After 10 years, maybe we will be able to compete. Maybe this basketball will make the rest of the world play better."

Competing against the best players every night builds your game and your confidence. You learn that the difference isn't as great as you think. The best players in any sport have an aura about them, and it isn't until you compete against them that you realize that if you work at it, you can close that gap.

That same idea was voiced by Marcel de Souza, a guard on the Brazilian team who says he wants to be a coach someday. "Today is one reality; 50 years from now will be another. There's only one way to improve: by playing guys better than you. I can't improve in Brazil, playing against guys who aren't any better."

Toni Kukoc of Croatia is a perfect example of such a player. I knew from having seen him before that he was a great player, a great shooter, a great passer, unselfish—he would fit in perfectly with any NBA team, especially the team he belongs to, the Chicago Bulls. He would be a perfect complement to the players they already have and to the style they play. He's a remarkable player, and he's only going to get better if he competes against the best.

Talent-wise we were clearly head and shoulders above every other team in Barcelona, and our reputation enhanced that margin. Only in the last game, one in which we came out a little flat, did we allow a team to hold a lead after the first minutes. But there was never any doubt about the outcome of any of the games that we played, including the final. I think that took a lit-

GERMAN TEAM MEM- BERS (ABOVE) THANK THE FANS FOR THEIR SUPPORT, WHILE (BELOW) ONE SPECTA- TOR DISPLAYS HIS ADMIRATION FOR THE U.S. TEAM'S TALENTS.

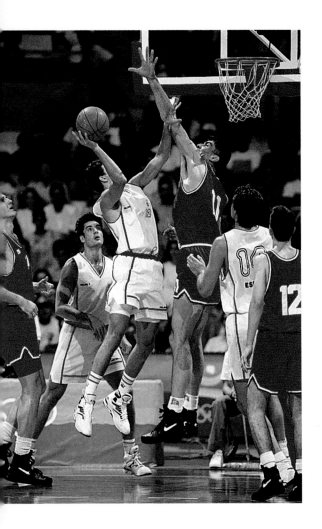

JORGE FERNANDEZ
OF SPAIN (NO. 11)
BLOCKS A SHOT
ATTEMPT BY
CROATIA'S ALAN
GREGOV.

tle bit of the edge off our feeling of achievement. As Larry Bird said in the interview room after the gold medal game, "We were never really challenged. Had we been challenged, it might have taken on more of a sense of accomplishment."

Had the teams from Yugoslavia and the Soviet Union, highly successful internationally in recent years, been able to remain together, and had we beaten them for the gold medal, it might have felt different. We'll never know.

I do know that if the team that won the 1990 World Championship, Yugoslavia, had been able to compete in the Olympics, we would have sweated bullets to win the final game. Croatia and Lithuania already are closer than many people want to believe, but because of the turmoil in their countries you can't really say when they'll be able to compete on a Dream Team level, if ever. There are many countries where the talent level is not there. Some are going to reach it, some aren't. The improvement will be gradual, over a period of years.

There will be considerable discussion about how the U.S. Olympic team should be chosen for 1996. I'll say this: if we want to continue to win the gold medal, we'd better be very careful to take top-flight personnel to Atlanta. Yes, I think we would have had a chance to win a gold medal this year with the collegiate group that was coming out, but only because it was unusually strong. With the early-entry rules in the NBA, most of the really great players don't last the full four years. And when you start looking at it on a year-by-year basis, I think it's going to be very hard to win the gold unless we take our top players—and that means NBA players. Even with the Dream Team, we often needed another dimension on a given night such as a Michael Jordan taking over, or a Scottie Pippen playing great defense, or a Larry Bird or a Chris Mullin hitting threes, or one of the other players to step up. The level of competition internationally is a little closer than these scores indicate, and it's only going to get closer.

Would a regular NBA team be able to win the Olympic gold medal? Probably, because I don't think even the best international teams, Croatia and Lithuania, are deep enough to compare with an NBA club. The problem might be a key injury. Let's say you had New York and Patrick Ewing got hurt early in a game or in the tournament. Then you would have a major problem because under Olympic rules you can't substitute a player on your roster due to injury. But in general, depth is the biggest problem the international teams have when you compare them to us. Wearing them down was part of our game plan. That's why we never called a time-out—why give them the extra rest?

Looking back on this experience, I honestly don't know what we could have done differently that would have produced a better result. There will always be controversy in selecting the team, but I think our selection committee did a great job. We withstood several injuries and still dominated.

One thing I would give serious thought to is naming the coach and players later. Naming the players after the first of the year might be better. I know USA Basketball said they had to do it in September because these guys needed to free up their schedules for the summer, but I think if they want to do it they can do it. And maybe naming the coach around All-Star time would work better. It might take some pressures off and make the task easier for an active NBA head coach.

You also have to be very cognizant of chronic injuries in making player selections, adding more people to the pool just in case some get hurt. This time we got away with it, but the fact is that we were without both our point guards for two full Olympic games and most of two others, which was pretty scary. I think there should be a pool of additional players, and then when the deadline for submitting the roster for the Olympics comes, you go in and pick 12. Otherwise you could fall short.

If the coach is going to continue not to have input into the

THE CHICAGO BULLS HOLD THE DRAFT RIGHTS TO TONI KUKOC (NO. 7) OF CROATIA, RATED BY MANY AS THE TOP PLAYER IN THE WORLD OUTSIDE THE NBA.

selection process, as was my case, I like the idea of choosing the players first and then naming the coach, which is the reverse order of what was done with the Dream Team. That might reduce the controversies that surround players from that coach's team not being on the Olympic squad—or being on it, for that matter. If he was an active NBA head coach, it would take a lot of pressure off him. For example, I had three players in Detroit who were of Dream Team caliber—Isiah Thomas, Joe Dumars, and Dennis Rodman—and at times it became sensitive, to say

PLAYERS GATHER IN THE SPARTAN LOCKER ROOM AT THE PALAU D'ESPORTS IN BADALONA FOR A BRIEF PRE-GAME MEETING.

the least. Having gone through it, I think this is a bigger problem than people realize, and it ought to be addressed before 1996.

Is the length of time we spent together enough? I truly think it was, for a team of veteran pros like ours. But for a team of collegians, or a team where half the players were collegians and half were pros, it might be beneficial to spend a longer period of time in training camp and to play more exhibition games.

I do want to say that this four-man coaching staff worked extremely well together, for which I think my three assistants—all successful head coaches in their own right—deserve the bulk of the credit. Lenny Wilkens has an outstanding demeanor and is a great communicator who could really relate and talk to the players if there were any problems. P. J. Carlesimo has the challenging personality of a class clown, but he's a solid basketball guy who was in charge of our scouting and always had us prepared. He was a valuable sounding board who kept reminding me about potential problems. And Mike Krzyzewski is a classic basketball man, probably one of the all-time great coaches, who knows the international scene very, very well (as does P. J.) and added valuable insight in meetings and on the floor.

I think I speak for all four coaches when I say we had a wonderful experience. It really couldn't have been any better for four major coaches, so to speak, to get along. We complemented each other very well.

There's a line Hall of Famer Red Holzman used to use when he was coach of the New York Knicks, although it's really an actor's line: "I come, I read the lines, I take the check, I go home." It sounds very simple, but there's a lot more to it than that.

So, that leads to the question everyone asks: would I coach the U.S. Olympic team again in 1996 if given the chance? Hey, that's easy. But four years is a long time away. More likely, four years from now as I sit and watch the next guy, I'll know what he's going through and I'll smile because I'll know it's not as easy as it looks.

APPENDIX

FOLLOWING ARE all-time rosters for both players and coaches who have represented the United States in the men's basketball competition at the Olympic Games; all-time results for the U.S. men's team; a medal summary table; year-by-year statistics for the U.S. men's teams; and complete box scores for games played by America's Dream Team at the 1992 Olympics.

All-Time U.S. Men's Olympic Basketball Roster

Name	Year	School	Name	Year	School	Name	Year	School
MARK AGUIRRE	1980	DEPAUL	PHIL FORD	1976	NORTH CAROLINA	FRANK MCCABE	1952	MARQUETTE
STEVE ALFORD	1984	INDIANA	JOE FORTENBERRY	1936	WICHITA STATE	PETE MCCAFFREY	1964	ST. LOUIS
WILLIE ANDERSON	1988	GEORGIA	CALVIN FOWLER	1968	ST. FRANCIS (PA)	TOM MCMILLEN	1972	MARYLAND
TATE ARMSTRONG	1976	DUKE	MARCUS FREIBERGER	1952	OKLAHOMA	RODNEY MCCRAY	1980	LOUISVILLE
JAY ARNETTE	1960	TEXAS	JOHN GIBBONS	1936	SOUTHWESTERN	ART MOLLNER	1936	LOS ANGELES J.C.
STACEY AUGMON	1988	UNLV	WAYNE GLASGOW	1952	OKLAHOMA	CHRIS MULLIN	1984, '92	ST. JOHN'S
SAM BALTER	1936	UCLA	JEFF GRAYER	1988	IOWA STATE	JEFF MULLINS	1964	DUKE
MIKE BANTOM	1972	ST. JOSEPH'S (PA)	ALEX GROZA	1948	KENTUCKY	SAM PERKINS	1984	NORTH CAROLINA
CLIFFORD BARKER	1948	KENTUCKY	ERNIE GRUNFELD	1976	TENNESSEE	DON PIPER	1936	UCLA
CHARLES BARKLEY	1992	AUBURN	BURDETTE HALDORSON	1956, '60	COLORADO	SCOTTIE PIPPEN	1992	CENTRAL ARKANSAS
DON BARKSDALE	1948	UCLA	BILL HANZLIK	1980	NOTRE DAME	DAN PIPPIN	1952	MISSOURI
JIM BARNES	1964	TEXAS WESTERN	HERSEY HAWKINS	1988	BRADLEY	R.C. PITTS	1948	ARKANSAS
MICHAEL BARRETT	1968	WEST VIRGINIA TECH	SPENCER HAYWOOD	1968	TRINIDAD J.C.	JACK RAGLAND	1936	WICHITA STATE
RALPH BEARD	1948	KENTUCKY	WALT HAZZARD	1964	UCLA	ED RATLEFF	1972	LONG BEACH STATE
LEWIS BECK	1948	OREGON STATE	TOM HENDERSON	1972	SAN JACINTO J.C.	J.R. REID	1988	NORTH CAROLINA
WALTER BELLAMY	1960	INDIANA	CHARLES HOAG	1952	KANSAS	JESSE RENICK	1948	OKLAHOMA STATE
LARRY BIRD	1992	INDIANA STATE	BILL HOSKET	1968	OHIO STATE	MITCH RICHMOND	1988	KANSAS STATE
RALPH BISHOP	1936	WASHINGTON	WILLIAM HOUGLAND	1952, '56	KANSAS	ALVIN ROBERTSON	1984	ARKANSAS
ROLANDO BLACKMAN	1980	KANSAS STATE	PHIL HUBBARD	1976	MICHIGAN	OSCAR ROBERTSON	1960	CINCINNATI
RONALD BONTEMPS	1952	ILLINOIS	DARRALL IMHOFF	1960	CALIFORNIA	DAVID ROBINSON	1988, '92	U.S. NAVAL ACADEMY
BOB BOOZER	1960	KANSAS STATE	LUCIOUS JACKSON	1964	PAN AMERICAN			
VINCE BORYLA	1948	DENVER	ROBERT JEANGERARD	1956	COLORADO	JACK ROBINSON	1948	BAYLOR
DICK BOUSHKA	1956	ST. LOUIS (CA)	EARVIN JOHNSON	1992	MICHIGAN STATE	KENNETH ROLLINS	1948	KENTUCKY
SAM BOWIE	1980	KENTUCKY	FRANCIS JOHNSON	1936	WICHITA STATE	BILL RUSSELL	1956	SAN FRANCISCO
BILL BRADLEY	1964	PRINCETON	BOBBY JONES	1972	NORTH CAROLINA	GLYNN SAULTERS	1968	NE LOUISIANA STATE
JIM BREWER	1972	MINNESOTA	DWIGHT JONES	1972	HOUSTON	WILLARD SCHMIDT	1936	CREIGHTON
MICHAEL BROOKS	1980	LASALLE	K.C. JONES	1956	SAN FRANCISCO	CHARLIE SCOTT	1968	NORTH CAROLINA
LARRY BROWN	1964	NORTH CAROLINA	WALLACE JONES	1948	KENTUCKY	STEVE SHEPPARD	1976	MARYLAND
QUINN BUCKNER	1976	INDIANA	MICHAEL JORDAN	1984, '92	NORTH CAROLINA	JERRY SHIPP	1964	SE OKLAHOMA STATE
TOMMY BURLESON	1972	N. CAROLINA STATE	KEVIN JOYCE	1972	SOUTH CAROLINA	CARL SHY	1936	UCLA
CARL CAIN	1956	IOWA	JOHN KELLER	1952	KANSAS	MIKE SILLIMAN	1968	U.S. MILITARY ACADEMY
JOE CALDWELL	1964	ARIZONA STATE	ALLEN KELLEY	1960	KANSAS			
GORDON CARPENTER	1948	KANSAS	MELVIN DEAN KELLEY	1952	KANSAS	ADRIAN SMITH	1960	KENTUCKY
KENNY CARR	1976	N. CAROLINA STATE	ROBERT KENNEY	1952	KANSAS	CHARLES D. SMITH	1988	PITTSBURGH
JOHN CLAWSON	1968	MICHIGAN	JAMES KING	1968	OKLAHOMA STATE	CHARLES E. SMITH	1988	GEORGETOWN
VERNELL COLES	1988	VIRGINIA TECH	JOE KLEINE	1984	ARKANSAS	KEN SPAIN	1968	HOUSTON
DOUG COLLINS	1972	ILLINOIS STATE	CARL KNOWLES	1936	UCLA	JOHN STOCKTON	1992	GONZAGA
MEL COUNTS	1964	OREGON STATE	JON KONCAK	1984	SOUTHERN METHODIST	DWAYNE SWANSON	1936	USC
ADRIAN DANTLEY	1976	NOTRE DAME	MITCH KUPCHAK	1976	NORTH CAROLINA	ISIAH THOMAS	1980	INDIANA
CHARLES DARLING	1956	IOWA	ROBERT KURLAND	1948, '52	OKLAHOMA STATE	WAYMAN TISDALE	1984	OKLAHOMA
RICHARD DAVIES	1964	LOUISIANA STATE	CHRISTIAN LAETTNER	1992	DUKE	RON TOMSIC	1956	STANFORD
KENNY DAVIS	1972	GEORGETOWN COLLEGE (KY)	TOM LAGARDE	1976	NORTH CAROLINA	JEFF TURNER	1984	VANDERBILT
			LESTER LANE	1960	OKLAHOMA	DARNELL VALENTINE	1980	KANSAS
WALTER DAVIS	1976	NORTH CAROLINA	WILLIAM LIENHARD	1952	KANSAS	DANNY VRANES	1980	UTAH
DONALD DEE	1968	ST. MARY OF THE PLAINS	ALTON LISTER	1980	ARIZONA STATE	JAMES WALSH	1956	STANFORD
			CLYDE LOVELLETTE	1952	KANSAS	JERRY WEST	1960	WEST VIRGINIA
TERRY DISCHINGER	1960	PURDUE	FRANK LUBIN	1936	UCLA	WILLIAM WHEATLEY	1936	KANSAS WESLEYAN
CLYDE DREXLER	1992	HOUSTON	JERRY LUCAS	1960	OHIO STATE	JOJO WHITE	1968	KANSAS
WILLIE EVANS	1956	KENTUCKY	RAY LUMPP	1948	NEW YORK U.	BUCK WILLIAMS	1980	MARYLAND
PATRICK EWING	1984, '92	GEORGETOWN	DAN MAJERLE	1988	CENTRAL MICHIGAN	HOWARD WILLIAMS	1952	PURDUE
VERN FLEMING	1984	GEORGIA	KARL MALONE	1992	LOUISIANA TECH	GEORGE WILSON	1964	CINCINNATI
JAMES FORBES	1972	TEXAS—EL PASO	DANNY MANNING	1988	KANSAS	AL WOOD	1980	NORTH CAROLINA
GILBERT FORD	1956	TEXAS	SCOTT MAY	1976	INDIANA	LEON WOOD	1984	CAL ST.—FULLERTON

USA All-Time Olympic Results (won 93, lost 2)

Angola (1-0)
116-48 — 1992

Argentina (2-0)
59-57 — 1948
85-76 — 1952

Australia (3-0)
78-45 — 1964
81-55 — 1972
78-49 — 1988

Brazil (8-0)
57-53 — 1952
113-51 — 1956
90-63 — 1960
86-53 — 1964
75-63 — 1968
61-54 — 1972
102-87 — 1988
127-83 — 1992

Bulgaria (1-0)
85-44 — 1956

Canada (5-0)
19-8 — 1936
95-77 — 1976
89-68 — 1984
78-59 — 1984
76-70 — 1988

Chile (1-0)
103-55 — 1952

China (2-0)
97-49 — 1984
108-57 — 1988

Croatia (2-0)
103-70 — 1992
117-85 — 1992

Cuba (1-0)
67-48 — 1972

Czechoslovakia (4-0)
53-28 — 1948
72-47 — 1952
66-35 — 1972
81-76 — 1976

Egypt (4-0)
66-28 — 1948
96-31 — 1972
*2-0 — 1976
102-35 — 1988

Estonia (1-0)
52-28 — 1936

F.R. Germany (1-0)
78-67 — 1984

Finland (1-0)
77-51 — 1964

France (3-0)
65-21 — 1948
36-21 — 1952
120-62 — 1984

Germany (1-0)
111-68 — 1992

Hungary (2-0)
66-48 — 1952
107-63 — 1960

Italy (5-0)
88-54 — 1960
112-81 — 1960
100-61 — 1968
68-38 — 1972
106-86 — 1976

Japan (3-0)
98-40 — 1956
125-66 — 1960
99-33 — 1972

Korea (1-0)
116-50 — 1964

Lithuania (1-0)
127-76 — 1992

Mexico (2-0)
25-10 — 1936
71-40 — 1948

Panama (1-0)
95-60 — 1968

Peru (2-0)
61-33 — 1948
60-45 — 1964

Philippines (3-0)
56-23 — 1936
121-53 — 1956
96-75 — 1968

Puerto Rico (5-0)
62-42 — 1964
61-56 — 1968
95-94 — 1976
94-57 — 1988
115-77 — 1992

Senegal (1-0)
93-36 — 1968

Soviet Union (5-2)
86-58 — 1952
85-55 — 1956
89-55 — 1956
81-57 — 1960
73-59 — 1964
50-51 — 1972
76-82 — 1988

Spain (7-0)
*2-0 — 1936
81-46 — 1968
72-56 — 1972
101-68 — 1984
96-65 — 1984
97-53 — 1988
122-81 — 1992

Switzerland (1-0)
86-21 — 1948

Thailand (1-0)
101-29 — 1956

Uruguay (6-0)
63-28 — 1948
57-44 — 1952
101-38 — 1956
108-50 — 1960
83-28 — 1964
104-68 — 1984

Yugoslavia (6-0)
104-42 — 1960
69-61 — 1964
73-58 — 1968
65-50 — 1968
112-93 — 1976
75-74 — 1976

*Game Forfeited

Men's Olympic Basketball Coaches Roster

Year	Head Coach	Assistant Coaches
1992	Chuck Daly	P. J. Carlesimo
		Mike Krzyzewski
		Lenny Wilkens
1988	John Thompson	Mary Fenlon
		George Raveling
1984	Bob Knight	Don Donoher
		George Raveling
1980	Dave Gavitt	Larry Brown
		Donald Roe
1976	Dean Smith	Bill Guthridge
		John Thompson
1972	Henry Iba	John Bach
		Don Haskins
1968	Henry Iba	Henry Vaughn
1964	Henry Iba	Henry Vaughn
1960	Pete Newell	Warren Womble
1956	Gerald Tucker	Bruce Drake
1952	John Womble	Forrest Allen
1948	Omar Browning	Adolph Rupp
1936	Jim Needles	Eugene Johnson

Men's Olympic Basketball Medal Summary

Country	Gold	Silver	Bronze	Total
United States	10	1	1	12
Soviet Union	2	4	3	9
Yugoslavia	1	3	1	5
Brazil	0	0	3	3
Uruguay	0	0	2	2
Canada	0	1	0	1
Croatia	0	1	0	1
France	0	1	0	1
Italy	0	1	0	1
Spain	0	1	0	1
Cuba	0	0	1	1
Lithuania	0	0	1	1
Mexico	0	0	1	1

Olympic Statistical History

1992—BARCELONA

	G	FGM-FGA	PCT	3PM-3PA	PCT	FTM-FTA	PCT	REB/AVG	PF	PTS/AVG	AST	BLK	STL
Christian Laettner	8	9-20	.450	2-6	.333	18-20	.900	20/2.5	11	38/4.8	3	3	8
David Robinson	8	27-47	.574	0-0	.000	18-26	.692	33/4.1	16	72/9.0	7	12	14
Patrick Ewing	8	33-53	.623	0-0	.000	10-16	.625	42/5.3	20	76/9.5	3	15	7
Larry Bird	8	25-48	.521	9-27	.333	8-10	.800	30/3.8	12	67/8.4	14	2	14
Scottie Pippen	8	28-47	.596	5-13	.385	11-15	.733	17/2.1	13	72/9.0	47	1	23
Michael Jordan	8	51-113	.451	4-19	.210	13-19	.684	19/2.4	14	119/14.9	38	4	37
Clyde Drexler	8	37-64	.578	6-21	.286	4-10	.400	24/3.0	14	84/10.5	29	2	19
Karl Malone	8	40-62	.645	0-0	.000	24-32	.750	42/5.3	10	104/13.0	9	5	12
John Stockton	4	4-4	.500	1-2	.500	2-3	.667	1/0.3	1	11/2.8	8	0	0
Chris Mullin	8	39-63	.619	14-26	.538	11-14	.786	13/1.6	12	103/12.9	29	2	14
Charles Barkley	8	59-83	.711	7-8	.875	19-26	.731	33/4.1	23	144/18.0	19	1	21
Magic Johnson	8	17-30	.567	6-13	.462	8-10	.800	14/2.3	3	48/8.0	33	0	8
USA TOTALS	8	369-638	.578	54-135	.400	146-201	.726	288/36	149	938/117.3	239	47	177

	G	FGM-FGA	PCT	3PM-3PA	PCT	FTM-FTA	PCT	REB/AVG	PF	PTS/AVG	AST	BLK	STL
1988—SEOUL													
Dan Majerle	8	48- 83	.578	6- 16	.375	11-18	.611	38/ 4.7		113/14.1	9	1	7
David Robinson	8	40- 69	.579	0- 0	—	22-30	.733	54/ 6.7		102/12.7	7	19	9
Danny Manning	8	40- 70	.571	0- 0	—	11-13	.846	48/ 6.0		91/11.3	6	3	5
Mitch Richmond	8	29- 60	.483	1- 4	.250	12-18	.667	27/ 3.3		71/ 8.9	17	0	10
Hersey Hawkins	4	11- 20	.555	5- 8	.625	8- 8	1.000	4/ 1.0		35/ 8.8	0	0	2
Charles E. Smith	8	28- 59	.474	4- 9	.444	9-11	.818	10/ 1.2		69/ 8.6	16	0	7
Charles D. Smith	8	23- 40	.575	0- 0	—	16-20	.800	23/ 2.8		62/ 7.7	2	6	1
Vernell Coles	8	23- 44	.522	0- 0	—	11-13	.846	14/ 1.7		57/ 7.1	7	0	11
Jeff Grayer	8	24- 45	.533	3- 6	.500	4- 9	.444	27/ 3.3		55/ 6.8	2	3	7
J.R. Reid	6	14- 30	.466	0- 0	—	8-13	.615	20/ 3.3		36/ 6.0	2	3	3
Willie Anderson	7	16- 25	.640	0- 2	—	3- 3	1.000	13/ 1.8		35/ 5.0	6	4	6
Stacey Augmon	6	3- 6	.500	0- 0	—	1- 2	.500	11/ 1.8		7/ 1.2	0	1	5
USA TOTALS	8	299-551	.543	19-45	.422	116-158	.734	299/37.4		733/91.6	74	40	73
1984—LOS ANGELES													
Michael Jordan	8	60-110	.545			17-25	.680	24/ 3.0		137/17.1	16	7	12
Chris Mullin	8	38- 67	.567			17-22	.772	20/ 2.5		93/11.6	24	3	14
Patrick Ewing	8	31- 56	.553			26-35	.742	45/ 5.6		88/11.0	4	18	6
Steve Alford	8	38- 59	.644			6- 7	.857	26/ 3.2		82/10.3	26	0	12
Wayman Tisdale	8	27- 50	.540			15-23	.652	51/ 6.4		69/ 8.6	3	7	6
Sam Perkins	8	29- 50	.580			7- 8	.875	43/ 8.4		65/ 8.1	10	5	7
Alvin Robertson	8	26- 40	.650			10-14	.714	22/ 2.7		62/ 7.7	20	0	17
Vern Fleming	7	23- 45	.511			8-17	.470	19/ 2.7		54/ 7.7	19	1	9
Leon Wood	8	14- 24	.583			19-24	.791	16/ 2.0		47/ 5.8	63	0	3
Joe Kleine	8	10- 16	.625			7- 8	.875	16/ 2.0		27/ 3.3	3	2	1
Jon Koncak	8	11- 25	.440			4- 8	.500	19/ 2.3		26/ 3.2	1	2	3
Jeff Turner	8	3- 15	.200			7- 9	.777	17/ 2.1		13/ 1.6	6	1	3
USA TOTALS	8	310-557	.556			143-200	.715	318/39.8		763/95.3	195	46	93

1980—The USA did not participate in the 1980 Moscow Olympics. However, the team did participate in the "Gold Medal Series" of games against NBA All-Stars in various USA cities. The cumulative statistics from the "Gold Medal Series" can be found below.

	G	FGM-FGA	PCT	3PM-3PA	PCT	FTM-FTA	PCT	REB/AVG	PF	PTS/AVG	AST	BLK	STL
Michael Brooks	6	29- 57	.509			21-32	.656	36/ 6.0	14	79/13.2	11	0	9
Sam Bowie	6	29- 49	.592			11-19	.579	41/ 6.9	12	69/11.8	12	14	0
Mark Aguirre	6	26- 54	.481			16-24	.667	30/ 5.0	14	68/11.3	16	1	9
Al Wood	6	27- 43	.628			6-12	.500	17/ 2.9	11	60/10.0	2	4	5
Isiah Thomas	6	22- 55	.400			14-17	.824	12/ 2.0	19	58/ 9.5	37	0	10
Rolando Blackman	6	22- 54	.407			4- 6	.667	28/ 4.7	5	48/ 8.0	14	1	5
Danny Vranes	6	17- 33	.515			7-11	.636	17/ 2.8	16	41/ 6.8	4	1	4
Darnell Valentine	6	14- 30	.467			6- 8	.750	12/ 2.0	4	34/ 5.7	17	1	14
Buck Williams	6	9- 23	.391			11-16	.688	24/ 4.0	8	29/ 4.9	5	4	3
Alton Lister	6	5- 14	.357			0- 0	.000	6/ 1.0	8	10/ 1.7	1	0	0
Bill Hanzlik	6	5- 14	.357			1- 3	.333	6/ 1.0	4	11/ 1.8	7	1	5
Rodney McCray	5	1- 3	.333			1- 2	.500	4/0.8	2	3/ 0.6	4	2	0
USA TOTALS	6	206-424	.476			98-150	.653	241/40.2	119	510/85.0	4	29	64
1976—MONTREAL													
Adrian Dantley	6	43- 80	.537			30-36	.833	34/ 5.6	12	116/19.3	10		
Scott May	6	42- 80	.525			16-18	.888	37/ 6.1	17	100/16.6	12		
Mitch Kupchak	6	30- 49	.612			15-20	.750	34/ 5.6	16	75/12.5	6		
Phil Ford	6	29- 54	.537			10-12	.833	13/ 2.2	17	68/11.3	54		
Quinn Buckner	6	22- 44	.500			0- 0	.000	18/ 3.0	19	44/ 7.3	18		
Kenny Carr	6	20- 36	.555			1- 2	.500	19/ 3.1	13	41/ 6.8	6		
Tom LaGarde	6	13- 18	.722			14-16	.875	11/ 1.8	18	40/ 6.6	1		
Phil Hubbard	6	12- 23	.521			4- 4	1.000	23/ 3.8	18	28/ 4.6	3		
Walter Davis	6	10- 21	.476			6- 6	1.000	10/ 1.6	14	26/ 4.3	12		
Ernie Grunfeld	6	9- 18	.500			3- 4	.750	4/ 0.6	9	21/ 3.5	15		
Mike Armstrong	6	5- 7	.714			6- 8	.667	2/ 0.3	0	16/ 2.6	2		
Steve Sheppard	6	3- 7	.428			3- 4	.750	6/ 1.0	2	9/ 0.6	1		
USA TOTALS	6	238-437	.544			108-130	.830	211/35.1	155	584/97.3	140		

1972—MUNICH

	G	FGM/FGA	PCT	FTM-FTA	PCT	REB/AVG	PF	PTS/AVG
Tom Henderson	9	39-74	.527	5-6	.833	18/2.0	20	83/ 9.2
Dwight Jones	9	34-68	.500	15-22	.681	51/5.6	26	83/ 9.2
Mike Bantom	9	29-72	.402	11-22	.500	44/4.8	33	69/ 7.6
Jim Brewer	9	26-62	.419	16-24	.667	64/7.1	20	68/ 7.5
Doug Collins	9	25-59	.423	16-22	.727	21/2.3	19	66/ 7.3
Tom McMillen	9	24-72	.333	13-16	.812	39/4.3	16	61/ 6.7
Ed Ratleff	9	27-68	.397	4-6	.667	29/3.2	26	58/ 6.4
Kevin Joyce	9	21-56	.375	6-6	1.000	11/1.2	28	48/ 5.3
James Forbes	9	23-45	.500	0-4	.000	28/3.1	18	46/ 5.1
Bobby Jones	9	14-23	.608	9-10	.900	25/2.7	14	37/ 4.1
Tommy Burleson	8	10-27	.370	7-12	.583	15/1.8	13	27/ 3.3
Ken Davis	8	6-18	.333	2-2	1.000	4/0.5	6	14/ 1.7
USA TOTALS	9	278-644	.428	104-152	.684	349/38.7	239	660/73.3

1968—MEXICO CITY

	G	FGM/FGA	PCT	FTM-FTA	PCT	REB/AVG	PF	PTS/AVG
Spencer Haywood	9	64- 89	.719	17- 38	.447		15	145/16.1
JoJo White	9	46- 98	.469	13- 16	.812		16	105/11.6
Mike Silliman	9	35- 78	.448	11- 12	.916		18	81/ 9.0
Charlie Scott	9	25- 49	.510	22- 32	.687		20	72/ 8.0
Bill Hosket	8	31- 49	.632	7- 16	.437		23	69/ 8.6
Calvin Fowler	9	26- 44	.590	6- 10	.600		24	58/ 6.4
Michael Barrett	9	26- 56	.462	4- 8	.500		17	56/ 6.2
Glynn Saulters	8	16- 30	.533	10- 10	1.000		9	42/ 5.3
Ken Spain	8	15- 17	.882	5- 14	.357		11	35/ 4.3
Donald Dee	7	13- 33	.393	7- 12	.583		13	33/ 4.7
John Clawson	8	13- 25	.520	3- 4	.750		9	29/ 3.6
James King	8	5- 10	.500	4- 6	.667		20	14/ 1.7
USA TOTALS	9	315-578	.544	109-178	.612		195	739/82.1

1964—TOKYO

	G	FGM/FGA	PCT	FTM-FTA	PCT	REB/AVG	PF	PTS/AVG
Jerry Shipp	9	52-102	.509	8- 10	.800		16	112/12.4
Bill Bradley	9	34- 66	.515	23-24	.958		29	91/10.1
Lucious Jackson	9	36- 75	.480	18-25	.720		20	90/10.0
Joe Caldwell	9	40- 80	.500	1- 6	.167		17	81/ 8.3
Jim Barnes	8	31- 58	.534	6- 12	.500		19	68/ 8.5
Mel Counts	8	22- 44	.500	9- 12	.750		17	53/ 6.6
George Wilson	8	15- 46	.326	13-19	.684		24	43/ 5.3
Pete McCaffrey	9	21- 42	.500	4- 6	.667		28	46/ 5.1
Larry Brown	9	14- 31	.451	9-10	.900		17	37/ 4.1
Walt Hazzard	9	14- 44	.318	6- 6	1.000		13	34/ 3.7
Richard Davies	9	11- 21	.523	9-14	.642		15	31/ 3.4
Jeff Mullins	8	8- 12	.667	2- 4	.500		6	18/ 2.2
USA TOTALS	9	298-626	.476	108-154	.701		213	704/75.5

1960—ROME

	G	FGM/FGA	PCT	FTM-FTA	PCT	REB/AVG	PF	PTS/AVG
Oscar Robertson	8	51-		34- 50	.680		24	136/17.0
Jerry Lucas	8	66-		4- 6	.667		23	136/17.0
Jerry West	8	46-		18- 27	.667		19	110/13.7
Terry Dischinger	8	37-		20- 29	.689		23	94/11.8
Adrian Smith	8	30-		27- 32	.844		19	87/10.9
Walter Bellamy	8	25-		13- 19	.684		32	63/ 7.9
Bob Boozer	8	23-		8- 13	.615		18	54/ 6.7
Lester Lane	8	20-		7- 9	.777		18	47/ 5.8
Darrall Imhoff	8	18-		2- 7	.286		22	38/ 4.7
Burdette Haldorson	8	11-		1- 4	.250		12	23/ 2.8
Jay Arnette	8	9-		5- 6	.833		16	23/ 2.8
Allen Kelley	5	2-		0- 0	—		11	4/ 0.5
USA TOTALS	8	338		139-202	688		233	815/101.8

1956—MELBOURNE

	G	FGM/FGA	PCT	FTM-FTA	PCT	REB/AVG	PF	PTS/AVG
Bill Russell	8	46- 96	.479	21- 27	.778		5	113/14.1
Bob Jeangerard	8	45- 74	.608	10- 11	.909		9	100/12.5
Ron Tomsic	8	34- 92	.370	21- 25	.840		12	89/11.1

	G	FGM/FGA	PCT	FTM-FTA	PCT	REB/AVG	PF	PTS/AVG
K. C. Jones	8	32- 75	.427	23- 27	.852		11	87/10.9
James Walsh	8	27- 61	.443	19- 21	.904		17	73/ 9.1
Burdette Haldorson	8	28- 58	.483	13- 15	.867		14	69/ 8.6
Dick Boushka	8	27- 68	.397	10- 10	1.000		12	64/ 8.0
Charles Darling	6	22- 44	.500	12- 15	.800		7	56/ 9.3
William Evans	8	21- 55	.382	12- 18	.667		11	54/ 6.8
William Hougland	8	20- 51	.392	6- 6	1.000		5	46/ 5.8
Gilbert Ford	8	17- 44	.386	5- 7	.714		14	39/ 4.9
Carl Cain	2	1- 5	.200	1- 2	.500		2	3/ 1.5
USA TOTALS	8	320-723	.456	153-184	.832		119	793/99.1

1952—HELSINKI

	G	FGM/FGA	PCT	FTM-FTA	PCT	REB/AVG	PF	PTS/AVG
Clyde Lovellette	7	39-		21-26	.769		21	99/14.1
Robert Kinney	7	27-		22-25	.714		14	76/10.8
Robert Kurland	7	24-		19-26	.730		19	67/ 9.6
Ronald Bontemps	8	16-		25-28	.893		11	57/ 7.1
Dan Pippin	8	23-		10-14	.714		18	56/ 7.0
Marcus Freiberger	7	15-		14-18	.778		25	44/ 6.3
William Hougland	8	20-		8-15	.533		19	48/ 6.0
Wayne Glasgow	6	10-		7-7	1.000		17	27/ 4.5
William Lienhard	4	5-		6-8	.750		12	16/ 4.0
Howard Williams	8	11-		5-9	.555		15	27/ 3.4
Frank McCabe	6	6-		6-9	.667		13	18/ 3.0
Charles Hoag	7	8-		4-6	.667		13	20/ 2.8
John Keller	2	1-		1-1	1.000		1	3/ 1.5
Melvin Kelley	6	1-		2-5	.400		10	4/ 0.7
USA TOTALS	8	206-		150-200	.750		210	562/70.3

1948—LONDON

	G	FGM/FGA	PCT	FTM-FTA	PCT	REB/AVG	PF	PTS/AVG
Clyde Lovellette	7	39-		21-26	.769		21	99/14.1
Alex Groza	7	35-		8-14	.571		19	78/13.0
Robert Kurland	7	27-		11-15	.733		17	65/ 9.2
R.C. Pitts	4	13-		5-6	.833		3	31/ 7.8
Don Barksdale	6	20-		14-19	.737		16	54/ 9.0
Raymond Lumpp	5	14-		8-10	.800		11	36/ 7.2
Wallace Jones	6	19-		5-9	.555		11	43/ 7.2
Gordon Carpenter	5	13-		9-12	.750		6	35/ 7.0
Vince Boryla	5	11-		6-10	.600		11	28/ 5.6
Jesse Renick	7	17-		5-7	.714		13	39/ 5.5
Lewis Beck	7	13-		7-11	.636		3	33/ 4.7
Kenneth Rollins	6	10-		4-5	.800		5	24/ 4.0
Clifford Barker	5	6-		5-12	.417		13	19/ 3.8
Ralph Beard	7	10-		6-12	.500		7	26/ 3.7
Jack Robinson	5	6-		1-3	.333		6	13/ 2.6
USA TOTALS	8	215-		94-145	.648		141	524/65.5

1936—BERLIN

	G	FGM/FGA	PCT	FTM-FTA	PCT	REB/AVG	PF	PTS/AVG
Joe Fortenberry	2	13-		3-				29/14.5
Frank Lubin	2	10-		2-				22/11.0
Francis Johnson	2	10-		0-				20/10.0
Sam Balter	2	8-		1-				17/ 8.5
Willard Schmidt	1	4-		0-				8/ 8.0
Carl Shy	2	5-		0-				10/ 5.0
William Wheatley	2	4-		1-				9/ 4.5
Jack Ragland	2	3-		1-				7/ 3.5
John Gibbons	1	3-		0-				6/ 3.0
Carl Knowles	2	2-		2-				6/ 3.0
Art Mollner	2	3-		0-				6/ 3.0
Don Piper	2	2-		0-				4/ 2.0
Dwayne Swanson	2	2-		0-				4/ 2.0
Ralph Bishop	2	2-		0-				4/ 2.0
USA TOTALS	4	71-		10-				152/38.0

GAME 1: JULY 26, 1992

ANGOLA (48)

	min	fg m-a	ft m-a	rb o-t	a	pf	pts
Sardinha	18	1-3	0-2	0-3	0	5	2
Macedo	25	4-7	0-2	0-2	0	3	10
Conceicao	33	2-13	4-7	2-7	2	3	10
Moreira	24	3-12	0-0	1-3	0	2	8
Dias	24	3-7	0-0	1-2	0	4	6
Victoriano	17	0-4	0-0	0-0	1	1	0
Wacuahambra	10	0-1	0-0	0-0	0	2	0
Coimbra	16	1-10	1-2	0-0	0	1	4
Sousa	19	2-8	0-0	0-0	0	2	5
Guimaraes	14	1-3	0-0	0-1	0	4	3
TOTALS	200	17-68	5-13	4-18	3	27	48

Percentages: FG-.250, FT-.385. Three-Point Goals: 9-38 .240 (Conceicao 2-4, Macedo 2-4, Moreira 2-8, Guimaraes 1-3, Sousa 1-6, Coimbra 1-9, Dias 0-1, Wacuahambra 0-1, Victoriano 0-2).

USA (116)

	min	fg m-a	ft m-a	rb o-t	a	pf	pts
Bird	16	4-5	0-0	0-3	0	0	9
Malone	19	7-10	5-7	2-3	1	1	19
Ewing	16	5-5	1-2	1-5	0	5	11
Johnson	19	1-2	4-4	0-2	10	0	6
Jordan	18	5-10	0-0	0-2	2	2	10
Laettner	10	2-3	3-4	0-3	0	0	7
Robinson	14	0-2	4-6	0-3	1	1	4
Pippen	21	1-3	3-4	0-0	5	1	5
Drexler	23	4-7	2-4	1-4	3	2	10
Mullin	22	4-7	2-2	1-2	3	1	11
Barkley	22	10-13	4-6	2-6	5	4	24
TOTALS	200	43-67	28-39	7-33	30	17	116

Percentages: FG-.642, FT-.718. Three-Point Goals: 2-9, .222 (Bird 1-1, Mullin 1-3, Laettner 0-1, Pippen 0-1, Drexler 0-1, Jordan 0-2).

ANGOLA	16	32	48
USA	64	52	116

GAME 2: JULY 27, 1992

USA (103)

	min	fg m-a	ft m-a	rb o-t	a	pf	pts
Pippen	28	5-9	2-4	1-2	9	1	13
Barkley	20	9-11	2-3	4-4	1	4	20
Robinson	14	1-3	1-1	0-3	0	4	3
Jordan	28	9-22	1-3	1-2	3	3	21
Johnson	9	1-2	2-2	0-3	1	0	4
Laettner	5	3-3	2-2	0-2	0	1	9
Ewing	12	1-2	0-0	1-2	0	2	2
Bird	19	1-5	0-0	0-3	1	2	3
Drexler	23	5-8	2-2	2-2	1	3	12
Malone	18	5-8	2-3	1-5	2	1	12
Mullin	24	0-3	4-5	0-1	6	2	4
TOTALS	200	40-76	18-25	10-29	24	23	103

Percentages: FG-.526, FT-.720, Three-Point Goals: 5-14, .357 (Jordan 2-5, Laettner 1-1, Pippen 1-2, Bird 1-3, Mullin 0-1, Drexler 0-2).

CROATIA (70)

	min	fg m-a	ft m-a	rb o-t	a	pf	pts
Kukoc	35	2-11	0-0	1-1	5	4	4
Radja	32	6-10	2-2	1-8	4	2	14
Vrankovic	30	2-3	7-8	0-8	3	1	11
Petrovic	35	6-16	4-9	0-3	3	4	19
Cvjeticanin	3	0-0	0-0	0-0	0	2	0
Perasovic	17	2-5	2-2	0-1	0	1	6
Alanaovic	5	0-0	0-0	0-0	0	0	0
Arapovic	3	0-0	0-0	0-0	0	2	0
Tabak	6	0-1	0-1	1-1	0	1	0
Gregov	4	0-1	0-0	0-0	0	1	0
Komazec	24	5-12	2-2	0-0	2	3	13
Naglic	6	1-3	1-2	0-0	1	0	3
TOTALS	200	24-62	18-26	3-22	18	22	70

Percentages: FG-.387, FT-.692, Three-Point Goals: 4-14, .286 (Petrovic 3-6, Komazec 1-5, Perasovic 0-1, Kukoc 0-1, Naglic 0-1).

USA	54	49	103
CROATIA	37	33	70

GAME 3: JULY 29, 1992

USA (111)

	min	fg m-a	ft m-a	rb o-t	a	pf	pts
Laettner	17	2-4	2-2	1-4	0	3	6
Robinson	19	4-6	1-2	1-4	1	0	9
Ewing	15	2-7	0-0	1-2	0	5	4
Bird	21	4-4	2-3	0-1	2	2	19
Pippen	18	2-2	0-0	0-2	6	2	4
Jordan	24	7-8	1-4	1-1	12	1	15
Drexler	18	4-8	0-0	0-1	4	2	9
Malone	20	8-10	2-2	0-5	6	1	18
Mullin	28	5-8	0-0	0-2	2	1	13
Barkley	20	6-11	2-2	2-3	1	2	14
TOTALS	200	44-68	10-15	6-25	4	17	111

Percentages: FG-.647, FT-.667, Three-Point Goals: 5-16, .312 (Bird 3-7, Mullin 1-2, Drexler 1-4, Pippen 0-1, Jordan 0-2).

GERMANY (68)

	min	fg m-a	ft m-a	rb o-t	a	pf	pts
Behnke	14	0-3	0-0	1-1	1	0	0
Rodl	19	1-1	2-3	0-0	2	1	4
Andres	5	0-1	0-0	0-0	0	1	0
Baeck	20	4-9	0-0	0-0	0	1	8
Neuhaus	4	2-2	0-0	1-1	0	0	4
Harnisch	24	2-9	3-4	2-3	1	4	8
Blab	15	2-6	0-2	7-2	1	2	4
Schrempf	34	5-12	4-5	2-8	2	2	15
Gnad	20	1-3	3-4	0-2	0	1	5
Nurnberger	16	2-3	0-0	0-0	1	0	5
Kujawa	7	0-1	0-0	0-0	0	1	0
Jackel	22	7-16	0-0	0-0	1	1	15
TOTALS	200	26-66	12-18	13-17	9	14	68

Percentages: FG-.394, FT-.667. Three-Point Goals: 4-16, .250 (Nurnberger 1-2, Harnisch 1-3, Schrempf 1-4, Jackel 1-4, Andres 0-1, Baeck 0-2).

USA	58	53	111
GERMANY	23	45	68

GAME 4: JULY 31, 1992

USA (127)

	min	fg m-a	ft m-a	rb o-t	a	pf	pts
Barkley	19	12-14	5-7	6-8	1	2	30
Bird	21	2-6	0-0	0-6	1	3	5
Robinson	15	5-8	1-1	2-3	3	4	11
Jordan	25	5-10	4-5	0-2	7	0	15
Drexler	28	4-9	0-4	5-7	10	1	8
Laettner	7	0-3	0-0	0-2	0	0	0
Ewing	23	5-8	3-3	4-9	2	0	13
Pippen	27	6-11	0-0	0-4	4	2	14
Malone	16	4-7	4-4	2-4	1	2	12
Mullin	19	7-12	2-3	0-1	5	4	19
TOTALS	200	50-88	18-27	19-46	34	18	127

Percentages: FG-.570, FT-.700, Three-Point Goals: 8-23, .350 (Mullin 3-5, Pippen 2-4, Barkley 1-1, Jordan 1-3, Bird 1-5, Laettner 0-2, Drexler 0-3).

BRAZIL (83)

	min	fg m-a	ft m-a	rb o-t	a	pf	pts
Schmidt	30	8-25	3-3	2-2	2	0	24
De Souza, Marcel	18	4-12	2-2	2-3	1	2	12
Victalino	16	1-5	0-2	1-5	0	4	2
Guerra	18	1-2	0-0	0-0	1	3	2
Machado	22	1-3	1-2	2-3	1	4	3
Boas	17	6-12	2-2	0-1	2	1	16
Viana	16	3-7	0-0	2-3	1	1	6
Ferreira	12	2-5	0-0	1-1	0	0	4
Cardoso	12	0-3	0-0	0-0	3	3	0
De Souza, Maury	14	0-1	0-0	0-1	7	2	0
Santos	14	5-6	2-4	3-9	0	1	12
Kuhn	11	0-2	0-0	0-0	3	1	2
TOTALS	200	31-83	12-17	13-28	21	22	83

Percentages: FG-.370, FT-.710. Three-Point Goals: 9-24, .380 (Schmidt 5-10, Boas 2-4, De Souza, Mar. 2-7, Cardoso 0-1, Viana 0-1, Victalino 0-1).

USA	60	67	127
BRAZIL	41	42	83

GAME 5: AUGUST 2, 1992
SPAIN (81)

	min	fg m-a	ft m-a	rb o-t	a	pf	pts
Jimenez	32	10-16	3-7	4-7	6	1	23
Herreros	23	2-5	2-3	2-2	2	1	6
Andreu	23	4-10	3-5	3-7	0	3	11
Villacampa	34	7-20	0-0	1-1	1	2	15
R. Jofresa	18	2-5	0-0	1-2	2	2	6
Arcega	11	1-2	2-2	0-1	0	0	5
Biriukov	11	1-6	2-2	0-0	0	2	4
Aldama	8	0-2	0-0	0-1	0	1	0
T. Jofresa	11	0-3	2-2	0-0	0	1	2
Fernandez	13	1-2	1-3	0-0	1	1	3
Orenga	16	3-8	0-0	1-4	2	3	6
TOTALS	200	31-79	15-24	12-25 14	17	22	81

Percentages: FG- .392, FT- .625, Three-Point Goals: 4-17, .235 (R.Jofresa 2-4, Arcega 1-2, Villacampa 1-3, T. Jofresa 0-1, Fernandez 0-1, Herreros 0-1, Andreu 0-1, Biriukov 0-4).

USA (122)

	min	fg m-a	ft m-a	rb o-t	a	pf	pts
Drexler	24	7-11	0-0	3-3	2	1	17
Malone	20	3-6	1-2	3-10	1	1	7
Robinson	14	4-8	1-2	3-3	1	4	9
Jordan	22	5-16	0-0	2-3	5	1	11
Mullin	20	6-11	0-0	1-2	1	2	14
Laettner	5	1-4	0-0	1-1	1	1	2
Ewing	20	6-7	2-2	3-10	1	3	14
Bird	20	5-9	2-2	0-4	3	3	14
Pippen	20	3-4	4-4	1-3	9	4	10
Stockton	6	1-2	1-2	0-0	0	0	4
Barkley	20	8-12	2-3	2-6	4	1	20
Johnson	9	0-1	0-0	0-0	1	0	0
TOTALS	200	49-91	13-17	19-45	29	21	122

Percentages: FG- .538, FT- .765, Three-Point Goals: 11-23, .478 (Drexler 3-3, Barkley 2-2, Mullin 2-5, Bird 2-5, Stockton 1-2, Jordan 1-3, Laettner 0-1, Pippen 0-1, Johnson 0-1).

SPAIN	35	46	81
USA	65	57	122

GAME 6: AUGUST 4, 1992 (QUARTERFINALS)
USA (115)

	min	fg m-a	ft m-a	rb o-t	a	pf	pts
Bird	18	3-8	0-0	2-5	1	0	7
Malone	15	5-9	2-3	1-4	0	3	12
Ewing	15	3-6	1-2	1-5	0	3	7
Johnson	22	5-8	0-1	0-3	7	1	13
Jordan	22	1-11	2-2	1-3	4	2	4
Laettner	11	1-3	8-8	3-8	1	3	11
Robinson	22	5-7	4-4	1-7	1	0	14
Pippen	22	5-7	0-0	0-3	8	1	12
Drexler	15	3-7	0-0	0-1	2	1	8
Stockton	6	0-1	0-0	0-0	6	0	0
Mullin	22	8-10	2-3	2-3	3	1	21
Barkley	10	2-4	2-2	0-1	2	5	6
TOTAL	200	41-81	21-25	11-43	35	20	115

Percentages: FG- .506, FT- .840, Three-Point Goals: 12-26, .462 (Mullin 3-5, Johnson 3-5, Pippen 2-3, Drexler 2-5, Laettner 1-1, Bird 1-5, Jordan 0-2).

PUERTO RICO (77)

	min	fg m-a	ft m-a	rb o-t	a	pf	pts
Ortiz	24	5-14	2-2	4-8	2	3	13
Lopez	16	0-4	0-0	0-1	0	0	0
Gause	7	1-6	0-0	0-0	0	0	3
Pellot	14	4-11	0-0	0-0	1	4	9
Mincy	19	0-7	0-0	1-3	1	2	0
Carter	19	2-8	1-2	0-2	4	1	6
Colon	15	1-5	0-0	0-0	1	4	3
Rivas	23	1-7	0-0	3-3	1	3	6
Morales	18	4-7	4-8	0-2	1	1	9
Deleon	19	5-7	1-2	2-3	0	3	11
Casiano	12	3-7	5-6	0-1	0	1	13
Soto	14	2-6	0-0	1-5	0	0	4
TOTALS	200	28-89	13-20	11-28	11	22	77

Percentages: FG- .315, FT- .650, Three-Point Goals: 8-28, .286 (Casiano 2-3, Morales 1-1, Ortiz 1-2, Carter 1-2, Pellot 1-3, Colon 1-4, Gause 1-6, Lopez 0-2, Mincy 0-5).

USA	67	48	115
PUERTO RICO	40	37	77

GAME 7: AUGUST 6, 1992 (SEMIFINALS)
LITHUANIA (76)

	min	fg m-a	ft m-a	rb o-t	a	pf	pts
Kurtinaitis	30	4-16	2-2	2-3	1	2	12
Karnisovas	13	3-5	2-2	1-1	0	4	10
Sabonis	23	4-17	2-2	2-8	2	2	11
Chomicius	21	0-5	0-0	0-2	2	1	0
Marciulionis	32	6-17	6-6	0-2	8	2	20
Pazdrazdis	11	1-1	0-0	0-2	1	4	3
Visockas	5	1-2	0-0	0-0	0	0	2
Dimavicius	13	1-2	0-0	0-1	0	1	2
Brazdauskis	14	0-0	0-0	0-3	0	1	0
Krapikas	14	2-3	0-0	0-0	1	0	5
Einikis	15	3-5	0-0	1-1	0	2	6
Jovaisa	9	1-3	2-4	0-0	0	1	5
TOTALS	200	26-76	14-16	6-23	15	20	76

Percentages: FG-.340, FT-.880, Three-Point Goals: 10-33, .300 (Karnisovas 2-3, Marciulionis 2-6, Kurtinaitis 2-9, Pazdrazdis 1-1, Krapikas 1-1, Jovaisa 1-3, Sabonis 1-5, Chomicius 0-5).

USA (127)

	min	fg m-a	ft m-a	rb o-t	a	pf	pts
Barkley	21	5-9	1-2	2-4	1	3	13
Pippen	11	1-4	0-1	0-1	2	0	2
Robinson	18	5-10	3-5	3-8	0	1	13
Johnson	21	6-8	0-0	1-3	8	1	14
Jordan	22	9-18	3-3	0-3	4	2	21
Laettner	4	0-0	1-2	0-0	1	3	1
Ewing	18	5-8	0-0	0-3	0	0	10
Bird	17	3-3	4-5	1-6	6	1	10
Drexler	19	5-7	0-0	1-3	4	2	10
Malone	19	7-10	4-7	3-7	1	1	18
Stockton	9	2-3	1-1	0-1	1	0	5
Mullin	21	4-6	0-0	0-1	1	1	10
TOTALS	200	52-86	17-26	11-40	29	15	127

Percentages: FG- .600, FT- .650, Three-Point Goals: 6-11, .550 (Barkley 2-2, Mullin 2-3, Johnson 2-4, Drexler 0-1, Pippen 0-1).

LITHUANIA	30	46	76
USA	49	78	127

GAME 8: AUGUST 8, 1992 (GOLD MEDAL GAME)
CROATIA (85)

	min	fg m-a	ft m-a	rb o-t	a	pf	pts
Kukoc	32	5-9	3-3	1-5	9	1	16
Radja	32	10-17	3-4	2-6	0	4	23
Vrankovic	17	0-3	0-0	0-1	0	4	0
Petrovic	36	8-17	5-7	1-1	5	1	24
Alanovic	24	0-4	0-0	1-1	1	1	0
Perasovic	11	2-3	0-0	0-0	2	3	6
Cvjeticanin	3	0-0	0-0	0-0	1	1	0
Arapovic	23	3-4	1-1	1-4	0	4	7
Tabak	5	0-3	0-0	1-1	0	2	0
Gregov	3	1-1	0-0	0-0	0	0	3
Komazec	8	1-1	2-2	0-0	0	1	4
Naglic	6	1-2	0-0	0-0	0	1	2
TOTALS	200	31-64	14-17	7-19	18	23	85

Percentages: FG- .484, FT- .824, Three-Point Goals: .530 (Petrovic 3-7, Perasovic 2-2, Kukoc 3-5, Alanovic 0-1, Gregov 1-1, Naglic 0-1).

USA (117)

	min	fg m-a	ft m-a	rb o-t	a	pf	pts
Malone	12	1-2	4-4	0-4	1	0	6
Pippen	23	5-6	2-2	2-2	4	2	12
Ewing	21	6-10	3-7	2-6	0	2	15
Johnson	28	4-9	2-3	1-3	6	1	11
Jordan	23	10-16	2-2	2-3	1	3	22
Laettner	2	0-0	2-2	0-0	0	0	2
Robinson	17	3-3	3-5	1-2	0	2	9
Bird	12	0-1	0-0	1-2	0	2	0
Drexler	20	5-7	0-0	1-3	3	2	10
Stockton	8	1-2	0-0	0-0	1	1	2
Mullin	17	4-4	1-1	0-1	4	0	11
Barkley	17	7-9	1-1	1-1	4	2	17
TOTALS	200	46-69	20-27	11-27	24	16	117

Percentages: FG- .667, FT- .741, Three-Point Goals: 5-13, .385 (Bird 0-1, Jordan 0-2, Drexler 0-2, Mullin 2-2, Barkley 2-3, Johnson 1-3).

CROATIA	42	43	85
USA	56	61	117

ACKNOWLEDGMENTS

THE AUTHORS WISH to thank Dave Gavitt, C. M. Newton, and Rod Thorn of USA Basketball for their license and cooperation throughout this endeavor; Lenny Wilkens, Mike Krzyzewski, and P. J. Carlesimo, fine head coaches all, for their total support and assistance; our fine medical staff of trainer Ed Lacerte and Drs. David Fischer, Stephen Lombardo, and Norman Scott; and all the dedicated support personnel from the USAB and NBA who worked long and hard behind the scenes to make the Dream Team a success. Thanks also to editor Alan Schwartz and Kathy Buttler, Michael Walsh, Karen Smith, Elaine Streithof, and Michael Reagan at Turner Publishing and to Bill Jemas, Frank Fochetta, Avonda Nelson-Perna, Renee Duff, Val Ackerman, Clare Martin, Mark Hurlman, Chris Brienza, Nicole Anderson, Lori Cook, Russ Granik, and David Stern at the NBA. Thanks go to the PR people who helped throughout, including Brian McIntyre, Terry Lyons, Josh Rosenfeld, and Barbara Colangelo of the NBA; Craig Miller and Amy Early of USA Basketball; Matt Dobek of the Detroit Pistons; and Vivian Lawand of Turner Publishing.

Last, and most important of all, out heartfelt thanks and appreciation to Terry and Cydney, Lori and Deborah, for their love, support, and inspiration.

Turner Publishing acknowledges the special help of the following people: James Porges, Laura Heald, Terry Davila, Rhonda Myers, Tammy Winter, Larry Larson, Craig Leachman, Virginia Pirie, Peri Koch, Bill Burke, Paul Van den bossche, Cecilia Harrington, Lori Jones, David Greenspan, Jane Lahr, Robin Aigner, Marcy Baron, Diane Joy, J. Stoll; the staff at Graphics International, including David Allen, J.C. Poole, Wes Aven, Lisa Davis, Jim Kennedy, Claudia McCue, Vicki Rumley, Tina Turner, and Kim Kiser; the staff at R.R. Donnelley & Sons, including Steve Neely, Debby Turoff, Bob Gospodarek, and Jerry Fletcher.